# NO
# BULL

# NO
# BULL

## My Life In and Out of Markets

Michael Steinhardt

John Wiley & Sons, Inc.

New York • Chichester • Weinheim • Brisbane • Singapore • Toronto

Published by John Wiley & Sons, Inc.
Published simultaneously in Canada.

This publication is designed to provide accurate and authoritative information in
regard to the subject matter covered. It is sold with the understanding that the
publisher is not engaged in rendering professional services. If professional advice or
other expert assistance is required, the services of a competent professional person
should be sought.

*Library of Congress Cataloging-in-Publication Data:*

Steinhardt, Michael.
    No bull : my life in and out of markets / Michael Steinhardt.
      p. cm.
    Includes index.
    ISBN 0-471-18152-8 (cloth : alk. paper)
    1. Steinhardt, Michael.   2. Capitalists and financiers–United States–Biography.
  3. Investments–United States.  I. Title.

HG172.S726 A3 2001
332.6′092–dc21
[B]
                                             00-069251

Printed in the United States of America.

10  9  8  7  6  5  4  3  2  1

To the greatest blessings of my life:
my wife, Judy; my children, David,
Daniel, and Sara; and my grandchildren,
be they many

# Acknowledgments

HIS MEMOIR WOULD NOT HAVE BEEN WRITTEN were it not for the determination of Karen Cook who, in addition to keeping a keen eye on my investments, managed to harass, cajole, humor, and in general intimidate me into writing it. For her tireless energy and persistence and, perhaps more important, with this book at long last completed, I truly thank her.

I am grateful to the people at Wiley, particularly my editor, Pamela van Giessen. Arthur Klebanoff of Scott Meredith Literary Agency was instrumental in getting this project off the ground and keeping it so. I would also like to thank Paul Alexander for providing early inspiration and guidance.

Lastly, I would like to thank my family, friends, and coworkers for their patience, insights, and even for their often ignored criticisms.

M. S.

# Contents

# CONTENTS

# NO
# BULL

# I

# THE PHONE CALL

OR SOME TIME, DURING MY EARLY FORTIES, I could not figure out why I often became depressed in the fall. Then I realized that this season was both the beginning and the end of a year for me. The school year started, and Rosh Hashanah, the Jewish New Year, followed, creating a feeling of hope, of new beginnings. But, before the Internal Revenue Service changed the rules for money managers and made the fiscal year coincide with the calendar year, my firm's fiscal year ended in September. Much of my life's focus has been on my performance as a hedge fund manager, and this focus took on a particular intensity as the close of the trading year approached. When my fiscal year ended each September 30, I felt a sense of closure and finality—the end of the play. Any good theatrical play has its beginning, middle, and end, or finale. My finale was September 30.

Fortunately, because I enjoyed success as a hedge fund manager throughout my career, September 30 was usually a good time. Congratulations, excitement, and joy filled the day. My investors, partners, and employees were happy. We often had superior performance—in some years, the best performance on Wall Street—and everyone usually made too much money.

But in October it all started again: the uncertainties, the insecurities, the worry about good performance. At the beginning of each new fiscal year, I had to start from scratch. What I, or any other money manager, had done in the past was soon "ancient history" because at the core of the competitive hedge fund world lurked a perennial question: "How much have you made for me this year?" or sometimes: "How much have you made for me this month? This week?" Each October, I felt a particular angst about having to start the performance all over again.

Traditionally, the window between the old and the new also provided an opportunity to take a short vacation. Things were no different in the fall of 1981.

After a brief visit to Israel, my wife Judy and I flew to the South of France, where we planned on staying at one of my favorite hotels, La Reserve de Beaulieu. The hotel appealed to me largely because of its cuisine. For me, dining is one of life's unmitigated pleasures. For days before arriving on the Côte d'Azure, I would fantasize about past meals: *scampi Provençale* with wonderful garlic aroma, the delicate *foie gras,* or the *loupe de mer* with fennel, which seemed to lift fish into an ethereal realm. This part of the world drew other people because of its scenic beauty (including the garb, or lack thereof, of the women), but the most exciting element for me was the menus. As Judy would remind me in her rare angry moments, I often had problems remembering details in more important areas of life, but when it came to menus, my facility for recall was outstanding.

We arrived in Beaulieu-sur-Mer late in the afternoon—happily, in time for the dinner hour. The flight had exhausted us so we decided to rest before our much anticipated culinary adventure. Just as we stretched out on the bed and began to enjoy the balmy October afternoon, the telephone rang. The hotel operator informed me that my assistant, Samantha, was calling from New York.

When I picked up the receiver, Sam, as I called her, told me she had received a call from an FBI agent. She gave me his number. He had told her to have me call him as soon as possible; she did not know why he was calling. It sounded urgent, so I said I would call him the minute we hung up. Before I got off the line, however, I asked to speak to one of my senior partners, John Levin. His first words to me, without even a hello, were: "Congratulations! The bonds have made a huge move. We're up 60 percent for the year." And the fiscal year had just started!

I knew the bond market had turned, but the magnitude of the move and its impact on our portfolio stunned me. Sitting on the side of the bed, I felt tremendous satisfaction in having been right, and having done so in an investment arena that was entirely new to me—the bond market. Since the age of 13, stocks had held a magical fascination for me. From amateur investor to professional, from analyst to trader to chief portfolio manager, my expertise had been in the stock market and my career had focused exclusively on stocks. The investment climate of the early 1980s, however, had created an extraordinary opportunity—better than any alternative, including stocks—in the bond market.

At the start of the 1980s, spiraling inflation, and the need to control it, plagued the U.S. economy. The federal government was running a huge deficit—enough to consume 2.5 percent of the nation's economic output. Long-term Treasury rates rose from about 10 percent in 1980 to almost 16 percent by September 1981. Short-term interest rates rose to 17 percent. Using "monetary policy"—mostly interest rate pressure—the chairman of the Federal Reserve, Paul Volcker, attempted to curb inflation but had had little success to date.

During the same period, Henry Kaufman, chief economist at Salomon Brothers (a man affectionately referred to as "Dr. Doom"), accentuated fixed-income fears with his dire predictions of record-high interest rates and runaway inflation. Most other economists on Wall Street were equally bearish on bonds—they referred to them as "certificates of confiscation"—and felt that inflation would continue to increase on both cyclical and secular bases. Oil prices were high and were predicted to continue rising.

I viewed things differently.

So, in the late spring, in the face of rapidly rising interest rates, I had begun a foray into the bond market. I started buying bonds on the premise that the economy would weaken faster than expected and would eventually cause a healthy drop in interest rates. Not only did I buy them; I bought them using leverage, or borrowed funds, thereby amplifying my risk. I was able to borrow extensively because, in contrast to equities, for which Federal Reserve margin requirements limited borrowing, only what a brokerage firm or bank would lend constrained the purchase of these government securities. Typically, one could get 95 to 99 percent of a bond's value. I saw an opportunity to earn compelling returns by borrowing most of the money to do so, albeit with a degree of leverage I had not used before.

In the early 1980s, I managed about $75 million in my two hedge funds—the flagship Steinhardt Partners, LP, and an offshore fund, SP International. Following my instincts, we invested $50 million of the funds' cash and borrowed another $200 million to buy a quarter of a billion dollars' worth of intermediate 10-year Treasury bonds. For a neophyte bond investor—indeed, by any measure—I had made a bold bet. But, given my history of superior performance investment, I felt confident that my judgment would be right.

∞

Eventually, my bond position grew to such a magnitude that, when I listed our major holdings in our monthly report to investors, the largest long position was U.S. Treasury bonds. I remained confident, even when the market moved against me, but I naively underestimated how my investors would react.

It was soon clear that my bet made many of my investors uncomfortable, especially since my entire history on Wall Street, until then, had been in the stock market. "What do you know about bonds?" investors queried. "I invested with you to be in stocks, not bonds." I heard that complaint over and over again.

Some clients grew so worried that they sent in redemption notices to withdraw their capital at the next available period. McKinsey & Company, the management consulting firm, was one such client. As soon as my monthly letter arrived, detailing my move into bonds, I was asked to meet with McKinsey's investment committee. Chosen from among the senior management of the firm, the committee was impressive and articulate, reflecting the fact that they had achieved their success by impressing other business leaders with their acumen.

When I explained why I thought bonds were attractive, they blasted me. "But you're an equity investor," the committee members kept saying. "We have you allocated as an equity manager. You cannot buy bonds." They redeemed their investment immediately following the meeting.

One Canadian investor went so far as to threaten to sue me over my bond position. "What do you know about bonds?" were the first words he yelled at me when he called one day. "You're an equity investor. You're supposed to be focused on the stock market. That's why I pay you these outrageous fees!" He did have a point. I had no experience in the bond market, hardly knew its mechanics or language, yet I had bet big against the consensus view that interest rates would rise, and bond prices would fall. The pressure of trying to pick a major turn, combined with this newfound investor dissatisfaction in an area where my own confidence was somewhat vulnerable, made for an emotionally wrought period. For a while, it looked as if my Canadian investor might be right.

Would my previous success in stocks translate into the same success in the fixed-income market? That's what my investors kept asking. My initial bond position was significant and, to make matters worse, I substantially increased that position as the months passed and the trade moved against me. There were some tough times. At one point, the fund suffered a $10 million paper loss.

∞

Given my history of outperforming the market and my intensely competitive personality, chaos ruled my life during the spring of 1981 as my financial fate went up and down (down more often than up) and I continued to accumulate bonds. A multiple of my capital, the bond position began to dominate the portfolio. If we had a bad month, our investors immediately brought up the bond exposure. I continually explained the rationale for taking such a huge position, but the interrogations were nonetheless unnerving. Moreover, the mechanics of dealing with leverage and timing a turn in interest rates were new to me and resulted in many sleepless nights.

Each week, I anxiously waited for the Federal Reserve to announce the money supply numbers, particularly M1 and M2, on Friday afternoon. Bonds bulls—investors like myself—hoped that the money supply would stop growing. This would indicate that the economy was slowing down and possibly heading into recession, good news for bondholders. I used my resources both within the firm and throughout the financial community to determine even a slight change in business. We gathered masses of anecdotal evidence, seeking signs of weakness. I even constructed my own New York City taxi index relating the percentage with "available" lights to those occupied, hoping for more to be "available," thereby signaling a slow-down in demand.

Bonds overwhelmingly influenced our results in the fiscal year that ended September 30, 1981. We posted a 10 percent gain compared to a decline of 3.5 percent for the Standard & Poor's (S&P) 500, but the volatility on a day-to-day, week-to-week, and month-to-month basis had been terribly high. I was relieved when the year ended. I could not wait to get away for a few days with Judy.

The phone call that afternoon, when John Levin informed me of the bond market's turn and our instant 60 percent gain, gave me a deep sense of satisfaction. I had been waiting for this turn all year, and now it had happened, almost overnight. As interest rates began to crack, the bond market shot up in price and our performance skyrocketed. It was one of the most gratifying moments in my financial life. I had put my money on what my instincts told me, and it had happened. My entire year had been made and we were not even past October. Our bond investment of $250 million, on $50 million of equity capital and the rest borrowed, made a profit of $40 million. We would eventually finish out the year up 97 percent, but my deepest feeling of gratification came at this particular moment, when I was proved right. I had found a new investment vehicle, losing some valued clients along the way, and I had felt the thrill of betting against the consensus and being lavishly rewarded.

I was elated when the call from the office ended, but I was still concerned because of Sam's message about the FBI agent. Who was Agent Bob Smith and why was he calling me? I called the number she had given me and got Agent Smith on the line. He told me there had been an armored-car robbery in Nanuet, New York, and several guards had been killed. The Black Panthers were responsible for the robbery, and the FBI, in its search for the perpetrators, had raided an apartment in

Newark, New Jersey. There they found, in addition to an arsenal of weapons, a cache of Panther literature that included a list of people the Black Panthers intended to assassinate. My name, Agent Smith told me, was on that list.

"We do not want to frighten you, Mr. Steinhardt," Agent Smith said, "but we felt it was our obligation to tell everyone whose name was on the list that they may be a target of this group."

"Who else is on the list?" I asked.

"It's a list of successful capitalists like yourself," the agent said. Since the Black Panthers were an anticapitalist, antiestablishment organization and its members had a history of espousing violence to achieve their goals, it made sense for the Panthers to have a hit list.

"There's really nothing you or the FBI can do about this," Smith said. "You should just know about it."

"I appreciate your telling me," I said, and I hung up the phone.

When I told Judy, she immediately wanted to go home to be with our children. It took me some time to persuade her that there was no reason to believe our kids were in danger. If anyone was going to be harmed, it would be me, and even that struck me as a remote possibility. After some anxious dialogue, we chose to finish our vacation.

Nothing ever came of the Black Panthers' hit list. Not long after Agent Smith's call, a number of Panthers were arrested, which may have squelched any real threat. But my getting those two pieces of information within minutes of each other—word from John Levin that my gamble on the bond market had paid off dramatically, and news from the FBI that, because of my visibility, I had become a target for assassination—stayed with me.

The confluence of those two phone conversations struck me as more than a coincidence. The first call validated my life as a hedge fund manager. I lived for the markets, and my investment expertise was now broadening to include areas beyond stocks. The second call made me realize how fragile life can be. No matter how successful I had become or would become, that success would never be permanent nor could I escape life's fortuities. In fact, my good fortune could bring problems of its own.

Here was a moment of unmitigated professional fulfillment—yet, as usual, I did not allow myself to bathe in reflective glory. The challenges of achieving the best performance constantly dominated my conscious being, but even when I realized a goal, as I had for most of my career, the joy was often fleeting and constrained. I was happier when pursuing success than I was when savoring its fruits; the attraction, perhaps the addiction, was in the process, as much as in its end. I reminded myself of Goethe's Faust, who always strove toward new goals rather than enjoying past achievements, and I wondered what might someday be more fulfilling than winning in the markets.

∞

In recent years, I have found a new purpose for my life. This is not to say that I have relinquished my fascination with markets. I still relish the risk taking and the rewards of a successful gamble, but I now know that such interests have limited psychic rewards, at least during this stage of my life. Unlike some other affluent people for whom the term "challenge" is associated with little more than a better golf score, I have sought an ennobled pursuit that would be, for me, compelling.

I am fortunate to have found a goal that seems to offer almost religious profundity. I do not believe in God, and the idea of a single "Absolute" holds no meaning for me, but creating a renaissance within the next generation of my people, the Jews, now dominates my conscious intensity as much as the markets once did. The objective is not just to "give something back," however commendable that may be. I have persuaded myself that even I, one individual, can have a positive impact on the future of one of the world's great peoples at a time when that future is, on many levels, clouded. For me, that goal holds tremendous meaning.

The value of the story in this book does not lie in my achievement of the American dream—at least the wealthy version of it. Many others have also achieved that and some more successfully than I. If anything, it lies in having found, in the middle of my life, a new passion that I, perhaps with a bit of delusion, can consider far more significant than making rich people richer. What I achieved in the markets was immensely valuable, but its true worth comes from my ability to pursue a particular philanthropic principle with the passion that I once dedicated to personal accumulation and the markets.

In most ways, I am no different from many others. I am the product of my Jewish immigrant heritage. I am the product of my parents: a mother who selflessly devoted herself to me, and a father who made an impression as an overpowering phantom figure throughout my life.

I cannot easily say how these modest beginnings impacted my perspective or my life. I am just one of thousands of Brooklyn Jews compelled to achieve, and that compulsion played out in the stock market, an institution that has transfixed me since childhood. By 1995, when I retired from active money management, I had achieved one of the most successful records on Wall Street. But my life could not have started out in a more unassuming fashion.

# 2

## BENSONHURST

**M**Y FATHER, SOL FRANK ("RED") STEINHARDT (AKA Red McGee), and my mother, Claire Dolleck, married in 1939. I was born in 1940. My parents divorced a year later, before I was a year old. I grew up with my mother in Bensonhurst, which was and still is a lower-middle-class section of Brooklyn. My father made occasional appearances. I never heard much about my parents' life together, probably because they did not *have* much of a life together. They had just enough of a union to produce me.

Throughout his life, my father was erratic and unpredictable. I never knew when he would appear or when he would once again disappear. In contrast, my mother was a rock. She was there when I needed her, and she did her best to be a mother *and* a father to me. My childhood may not have been ideal, but I did not realize its flaws most of the time. The credit for that goes to my mother.

My father grew up in the 1920s in Brownsville, one of Brooklyn's toughest neighborhoods. Its residents are mostly black now but in those days poor Jewish immigrants lived there. His mother and father each had three children from previous marriages before they met. Then they married and had three children together. My father was the middle child of those

15

last three, which meant he had six half brothers and sisters, a full brother, and a full sister, all of whom are now deceased.

My paternal grandfather died before I was born. In the pictures I have of him, he looks as if he just rode in off the Russian steppes. He had a Mongol, almost Oriental, appearance, and we can trace his early life back to the Ukraine. My paternal grandmother died when I was five years old. She was a beautiful redheaded woman. My father's nickname, Reuta (Yiddish for "Red"), came from his having the same bright red hair as his mother.

My mother took my father's last name, Steinhardt, when they married and kept it until she remarried many years later. The Steinhardt name itself is of German ancestry; indeed, there is a small town in the Rhineland called Steinhardt. Consequently, most Steinhardts in America can trace their ancestry to Germany. A well-known aquarium in San Francisco even bears the name. I have sometimes said jokingly that the bright Steinhardts left Germany and went west. My forebears probably went east to Russia before realizing their mistake and heading to America.

My father dropped out of school at age 12 and supported himself with whatever jobs he could get. He often worked as a manual laborer. Sometimes he and his brother, Bernie, put up awnings and venetian blinds to earn money. Early in life, my father was hardworking, but, unlike many of his era, he was not committed to saving so he spent or gambled away all that he made. Like many of the "role models" in his neighborhood, he loved gambling. He was an avid gambler from a young age. He bet on horses and sporting events, played in crap games, legal and otherwise, and played card games, especially clobyosh, a game favored by Eastern European immigrants, with all sorts of wise guys.

His chronic gambling became a problem, at least as far as my mother was concerned. Later in life, my mother told me that, during the one year they were together, my father sometimes came home with money to pay the rent and other bills but, more often than not, his pockets were empty. From the start, he was not reliable, and she frequently did not have enough cash for groceries. It was because her life with my father was so insecure that, after living with him for only a few months, she moved back to her parents' house. This, in effect, ended their marriage.

In those days, divorce was a disgrace, especially in Jewish families. But as I grew up, I did not feel at all humiliated or stigmatized by my parents' divorce. I just knew that my family's circumstances were different from those of my friends and schoolmates. While my friends' fathers would sometimes show up at school events such as class plays, sporting contests, or parent-teacher meetings, my father was never there, just my mother. This did not bother me much, although I sometimes missed him on weekends when my friends played ball with their fathers. I never had the experience of tossing a baseball back and forth with my father.

❦

I grew up in an apartment in Bensonhurst: 2169 Seventy-second Street, between Twenty-first Avenue and Bay Parkway. Our apartment was a second-floor walk-up in a building with four apartments—two on the first floor and two on the second. It had a living room, a dining room, a kitchen, two bedrooms, and a bathroom. Our living conditions were modest. Indeed, economically, the neighborhood was first- and second-generation immigrant, lower middle class, yet we thought we were better off than we actually were. Throughout my childhood, my mother worked as a bookkeeper for my Uncle Louie, who owned a wholesale fruit business, specializing in selling apples, on Manhattan's Lower West Side. (Later, the wholesale fruit business district moved to Hunts Point, in the Bronx, where it remains today.) Money may never have been plentiful (my first bicycle was a used two-wheeler), but every month the rent got paid.

Most months, my father gave my mother $50, always in cash, to supplement her income, as ordered by the divorce court. The arrival of my father's child-support payments was almost as unpredictable as his sporadic visits. Not too many months would go by without a visit or a payment, but we never knew exactly when they would arrive. The $50 came in handy, but it was rarely enough. When my mother needed help, she turned to her brother, my Uncle Sol, who had a senior job at the Census Bureau in Washington, D.C. He was always willing to chip in if we needed a little extra cash.

My mother's parents lived with us. Or rather, we lived with them; it was their apartment. When I was four, my grandfather died of a heart attack. Then only my grandmother, who spoke mostly Yiddish, was there to help my mother raise me. Because my mother was one of the few women in our neighborhood who worked, my grandmother was often the only person in the house when I came home from school. I had a happy childhood, primarily because of my mother, but also thanks to my grandmother.

In the 1940s, Bensonhurst was a real "street" neighborhood. Stickball was played amidst the traffic, using the manhole covers as bases. In warm weather, neighbors sat on their stoops and gossiped with each other, and the sounds of radios drifted out from the open windows of the row houses. Except for rare excursions, most of my early life was lived within a few short blocks of home.

There were a few exceptions. When we could afford it, my mother took me on vacation to the Catskill Mountains, a popular summer-resort destination sometimes referred to as "the Jewish Alps." We stayed in a modest lakeside bungalow or a family-style hotel. Before my voice changed, I competed in guest talent shows, singing "I'd Love to Get You on a Slow Boat to China" and Nat King Cole's classic, "Because of You." No talent scouts approached me, but my mother thought I was tops. She and I also fished in the mountain lakes. I hated to hook the worms, so my mother used to bait them for me, even though she found this slimy chore as unappealing as I did.

I enjoyed the vacations, but I really *loved* Bensonhurst, *my* neighborhood! I knew my way around all the streets and stores as well as I knew my own apartment. There was Kitzy's candy store; the Sweet Box, where my friends and I drank egg creams and milkshakes; and Smolinsky's Kosher Deli, where we ate Romanian tenderloin steak and kishka. I loved walking down the streets, playing ball between the cars, talking to people in the stores. It seemed I knew everybody in my neighborhood and they all knew me. Occasionally, I had scuffles with other kids, but I could not have felt more secure. I adored Bensonhurst; I thought I would live there for my entire life.

In those days, Bensonhurst was a mix of Jews and Italians, with somewhat more Jews. Jewish fathers often worked in the garment and fur trade or as civil servants. The Italians were mostly tradesmen—plumbers and electricians. Most of my friends were Jewish, but I knew lots of Italians as well. Over the years, Bensonhurst did not change much. The Jews often attributed this stability to our Italian neighbors' fabled Mafia connections. This speculation remained unproven, but it certainly allowed the Italian kids to intimidate us.

For years, I had the same group of friends with whom I endlessly played games. George Henry, who would later join me as an economist at Steinhardt Partners, was my earliest best friend until he moved from the neighborhood when I was nine years old. Every day after school, I'd play some ball game: stickball, softball, football, punchball, triangle, curves, hit-the-penny, Chinese handball, and so on. For a brief time, I played in the basketball league at the Jewish Community House.

During those early years, I developed a love of baseball and became an avid New York Giants fan—pretty unusual for a kid from Brooklyn, where almost everyone was a Dodgers fan. Perhaps this was the first example of my future propensity to go against conventional wisdom. Taking me to see Giants' doubleheaders at the Polo Grounds, all the way up on 158th Street in Manhattan, was more than a little inconvenient for my mother. It required a long, hot subway ride that included at least one transfer and lasted over an hour. My mother had no interest in baseball, but she took me anyway. For me, a Sunday Giants' doubleheader was the ultimate way to spend an afternoon. Looking back, I am not sure why I became a Giants fan. Maybe it was because the Yankees were so successful and being one of their fans seemed irrelevant. They did not need me. Then again, maybe I just wanted to be different, individualistic.

I sometimes fantasized about being a great athlete, but I had to settle for solid mediocrity. I did, however, have a few brief moments of athletic glory. In junior high, I played in an inter-class softball league. On one afternoon I will never forget, we played the ninth-grade jocks, who were mostly Italians. They slaughtered us because they were a year older and were much, much better players. I played third base and, at one point, a slugger hit the ball high over the head of our center fielder. As the batter loped around the bases, our center fielder ran back, got the ball, and relayed it to the shortstop in shallow center field. The shortstop turned and fired the ball to me as the runner rounded second base. This jock, suddenly realizing he could not lope any longer, charged me, really picking up speed. I knew he and the ball were going to arrive at approximately the same time. I also knew he was going to clobber me. But I stood there, put my glove out, caught the ball, tagged him, and got slammed. He was called out. That was just about my only memorable athletic feat in a rarely distinguished career.

Years later, I was reading about the murder of a man in Bensonhurst as he walked out of a liquor store. A hit man had been waiting for him, the two started to shoot it out, and the target, a guy named Ralph Ronga, was killed. He was the jock who had slammed into me that day on the softball field. In later years, he had lived a crime-ridden life, proving some of the neighborhood gossip correct.

My best friends, from a young age on, were Irwin, Marty, and Kitzy. We were close back then and I am still friendly with them today, even though our lives have taken separate paths. Irwin is now a psychoanalyst. In our annual "boys'" weekend away, he joyfully relives the athletic moments of our youth. Marty, a dental research scientist, now fishes at Cape Cod as we once fished at Sheepshead Bay. Kitzy, also known as Steven Kitzes, a social worker, was the proud scion of the neighborhood candy store. Those three chums helped to define my youth during a time when Bensonhurst—indeed, all of Brooklyn—was one big neighborhood and boys like us could spend a whole day entertaining themselves by trading baseball cards on someone's stoop or playing touch football in the street.

∞

Most of my friends' parents, like mine, had had no college education. Indeed, some had never finished high school. But, as in other traditional Jewish families, our parents emphasized education as the means toward social advancement. Thus, we Jewish children of Bensonhurst wanted to become doctors and lawyers and accountants.

Being one of the bright Jewish kids, I went through Seth Low Junior High School in two years. Anyone with an IQ exceeding 130 followed a curriculum called "SP" (Special Program). This group, made up mostly of Jews, was allowed to skip from the seventh to the ninth grade. I made most of my teenage friends in this group.

After Seth Low, I attended Lafayette High School, near Coney Island, a relatively new high school at the time. The school reflected my neighborhood—about half Jewish and half Italian—but I never developed a deep affection for it. The quality of teaching was erratic, but my intellectual horizons broadened at Lafayette. I particularly remember Mr. Feldman, my social studies teacher, who first introduced us to politics and economics. He was five feet high and five feet wide—a singularly intimidating teacher because he did not tolerate stupid questions. He conveyed his own intense commitment to the subject matter and left me with a lifelong interest as well.

Lafayette had a strong athletic program, but I went through my three years there without participating in or attending any athletic events. My sports days were behind me. I also passed through high school with few other involvements, rarely participating in extracurricular activities; I was simply not interested. Partially as a result, I did not make many new friends. Instead, I stuck with the same group I had hung around with since the SP at Seth Low. I also did not spend much time with girls and no doubt suffered from being one year younger than my classmates. I admired, even envied, classmates who dated and were socially active, but my socialization was confined to rare parties where we played Spin the Bottle.

❧

In addition to our secular education, I, and most of the other Jewish kids, went to Hebrew school. While I loved almost all the other aspects of my life, my Hebrew education was an abject failure. When I was a child, the synagogue impressed me only as the Land of Smelling Salts. On Yom Kippur, elderly men would pass these salts around to revive themselves from the fast. To me, the salts were emblematic of the soporific tone of the service itself, with its stuffiness and Old World qualities.

22

I attended B'nai Isaac, an Orthodox synagogue, which suffered the same doldrums that had already seeped into many synagogues throughout America. The only positive memory I have involves throwing chickpeas around on Simchat Torah—hardly a religious epiphany.

Being young and impatient with archaic traditions, I often acted as the wise guy. In Hebrew school, which I grudgingly attended five days a week, the rabbi came in one day and boasted, "The Torah deals with everything. You name it. Any subject that enters your mind."

I leaned toward a friend and whispered (quite ignorantly, I now realize): "I'll bet the Torah does not discuss pubic hair."

The rabbi said, "Michael! What did you say?" I was too embarrassed to repeat my comment. Today, I remain in touch with that same rabbi, P. H. Singer, toward whom I feel great affection.

Everything about B'nai Isaac struck me as Old World, out of touch with the excitement of the American culture I experienced every day. The Hebrew school enrolled only boys, impinged on free time, offered poor teaching from an immigrant staff, and had a negligible reward system for doing well. Even the Hebrew language instruction was dreary. Instead of learning the modern idiom of the fledgling State of Israel, we learned an Ashkenazic version of ancient Hebrew prayer books. There was no joy. All told, it was enough to make my lackluster public high school seem exhilarating. I played hooky whenever I could, but this was not without its risks. Once, when my mother came home from work early, she caught me and chased me under my bed with a broomstick.

Yet, my mother was not observant herself. Like many women of her generation, she had little education in Jewish tradition but tried to maintain its basics. My Jewish upbringing might best be described as nominally Orthodox. We kept a kosher home, observed Rosh Hashanah, and held Passover Seders. During the years my grandmother was alive, we lit Shabbat candles on Friday night. Hanukkah was a time of gift giving, and we kept Yom Kippur sacrosanct by fasting, not using electricity, and wearing cloth sneakers instead of leather shoes. To this day, I am not sure why.

Yom Kippur was the most intense holiday. The experience of fasting fostered excited teenage discussions of the challenge of dealing with hunger, but hardly imprinted any spiritual context or significance. As the afternoon wore on, there was a sense of accomplishment from the fast and a certain giddiness in the synagogue. At nightfall, the shofar was blown, creating a profound moment and ending the fast. Though my mother urged my grandmother to ignore the fast in the last years of her life (she was in failing health), she steadfastly refused.

Some religious events did have an impact on me. I remember that as my Bar Mitzvah approached, my grandmother became sicker, and it was clear that her time was limited. At the Bar Mitzvah service itself, I was not sure she would make it to the synagogue. Finally, just as I was about to read my Haftorah portion, she walked in slowly, leaning on my mother's arm. My mother was big boned and three or four inches taller than my grandmother Rae (her full name was Rachel), who was delicately thin. She looked like an apparition, with her pure white hair and her extraordinarily pale, even luminescent, skin. The whole congregation stopped to look at her, whispering of her beauty. That was the last time I saw my grandmother walk. She died a month later.

My family kept the vestiges of Jewish religious life intact but did not communicate its virtue to me. Much of my neighborhood felt the same way. When one wanted to disparage a fellow Jew, he would call him a "greenhorn" or a "mocky," suggesting he was inexperienced in the ways of America. Religious observance was associated with the old or those new to the country. People anglicized their names, the more American, the better. Many Jews who otherwise kept kosher homes frequented local Chinese restaurants and engaged in other conflictual behavior. Soon after my grandmother died, we even started bringing Chinese food inside our home.

Most of my positive religious experiences came from a humbler place than my synagogue. For a few years before my Bar Mitzvah, I accompanied my close friend, Marty Taubman, to a *shtiebl* (a small, makeshift place for prayer) tucked inside the basement of a Bensonhurst tenement. We started going there because Marty's grandfather prayed there. He and other old men, wearing long prayer shawls and rocking back and forth, surrounded us. This place had a different atmosphere than B'nai Isaac. The big synagogue service was rote and somnambulant; the small *shul* was warm, zesty, and even touching, though the disparate prayer books were only in Hebrew, which I could not understand. There was never enough money to buy one uniform set that had an English translation. Yet, in contrast to the synagogue, the *shul*'s energy was only enhanced by its unabashed Old Worldliness. Marty and I were the only kids present, aside from the rabbi's son, but the old men looked forward to our presence. They welcomed us. We just sat in the back yapping during the service and occasionally were offered *aliyahs* (being called up for a portion of a torah reading). For some reason a peculiar feeling of community existed. While both B'nai Isaac and the *shtiebl* were remnants of the same Old World, something about the atmosphere of the small *shtiebl* called to me in a familiar voice.

My encounters with Judaism did not end with the synagogue and *shtiebl*. From my earliest days, I would run into neighbors who had numbers tattooed on their arms. These refugees from the Holocaust—some of them my own age— were often lame or disfigured. The sight of them had a profound effect on me. I had been taught Biblical stories of

Divine providence in which God personally intervened to save and reward the good and to punish the wicked. But, as I got older, I began to read Holocaust memoirs that described a world of absolute moral chaos. I asked myself: In the most awesome tragedy to ever befall the Jewish people, where was God?

I perceived a dissonance between the theological explanations of a just God dispensed at synagogue and the empirical evidence of what had occurred in my own lifetime. Where was God in the age of Auschwitz? The world's most respected rabbis explained it by saying: "We cannot explain it. Some things are beyond the human mind's ability to grasp." This seemed a theological cop-out, a call to blind faith, and it could not assuage my conflict.

By the time I was in high school, it became difficult for me to accept, with my naïve teenage logic, the existence of a Jewish God. It made more sense to conclude that this was a world in which one's experience should be the dominant force. The higher I pursued my secular education, with its explorations into philosophical logic, science, and mathematics, the more I became convinced that religious tradition was rooted in mythology. Biblical accounts of the creation of the world did not seem dissimilar from the folklore of primitive societies I learned about in anthropology courses at college. It was a sad awakening for me because it suggested that the religious story and prayers of generation after generation of Jews contained little that verified "chosen-ness."

Jewish tradition, like most religions, brims with tales of miracles. The fact that neither I nor anyone I trusted had personal knowledge of a miracle, or of any sort of credible divine intervention, made it difficult for me to abide by the precepts of our faith. Indeed, I linked my rejection of all that is supernatural with much of what was read every week in the synagogue.

But there was one miracle in my childhood, one spiritual moment of human heroism that perhaps reached a divine level.

This miracle made much of my doubt happily recede. I am referring to the creation of the State of Israel.

∞

The establishment of Israel and the effort to defend her had a profound impact on me. Tormented by the Holocaust, I found solace in daily reports of the Jewish people rising like a phoenix from the ashes.

From my earliest memories, Israel caused hope and joy but also brought anxieties. I cannot exaggerate my visceral bonds to Israel. During my teenage years, I pored through the weekly edition of the *Jerusalem Post*. When Israel's security was especially threatened, it was as if my own person was threatened. Whether France would sell advanced jet fighters to Israel took on an exaggerated significance.

I accepted all the Zionist propaganda and therefore worried about things like the possibility that the Sea of Galilee would go dry. Israel routinely reported on its water level, its red line, and it always seemed to be on the verge of drying up. I feared the day might come when someone in Jerusalem would go into the kitchen, turn on the tap, and instead of water there would be three brownish drops. Plop, plop, plop.

I wanted to be part of this national rebirth, and I had elaborate fantasies about holding off Arab hordes to protect a vital hill or a settlement. I dreamed about the small, outnumbered, underdog country that, through skill and courage, overcame a larger, evil enemy bent on destroying her. I was receptive to the prevalent allusions to David versus Goliath. Contemporary cinema also influenced part of this fantasy life. One film, *Hill 24 Doesn't Answer,* lacked much artistic merit, yet its images had a lasting effect on me. It depicted a group sent to defend a hill that was considered crucial in carving out the borders after the imminent cease-fire between Israel and its adversaries in the War of Independence. In the end, all the defenders on the hill were killed. But, when the United Nations' partition people came and saw the bodies of those who had defended Israel's border, they declared the hill to be within the newly created boundary of the state. In my youthful fantasies, enacted in the shelter of America, to die such a death was a noble act.

Yet, Israel alone was not enough to ameliorate my crisis of faith. Over the years, I have often directly confronted my conflicts of belief, whether by attending services, studying the Torah and Talmud, or speaking with esteemed rabbis. I have even started collecting Judaica, with the perspective that perhaps this connection to sacred objects of Jewish tradition might illuminate faith for me. Nothing has been able to bridge the gap.

I have realized, however, that Jewish identity can be powerful without necessarily hinging on one's belief in God. Culture, values, and peoplehood are perhaps even more powerful sources of Jewish identity. I understand only a few words of Yiddish, but I love the sound of the language. When I hear Klezmer music, I am emotionally stirred. It is as if some part of me or of a former me has always known the words. The music of pre-World War II Eastern European Jewry has, for me, a resonance that I cannot explain. It pains me that little serious effort is being made to transmit this vibrant Jewish culture to future generations. Jewish values, whether or not evolved out of Divine fiat, are compelling enough not only to have sustained our people through thousands of years, but to have allowed us to make disproportionate contributions to the world's civilization. Even though I struggled with it, and continue to struggle with it, it is, for me, an important tradition that should be passed on to future generations.

The seeming inconsistency of my atheism and my intense commitments to the Jewish future perplexes many people, particularly committed Jews. Indeed, some of the rabbis with whom I work most closely, affectionately mock my self-proclaimed atheism and insist that whatever I say, I am a believer. To me, however, I have made a higher form of commitment that does not require a supernatural being who rewards and punishes and from whom values emerge. Instead, I am one who cherishes Jewish history, all of Jewish history, and takes pride in this people that have endured with or without God's help. The heroism is all human. The suffering is all human, and while belief has played an important role over the centuries, it is the human achievement, not the belief, that I revere.

Thus the Jewish attribute I cherish most highly is my sense of peoplehood. My love for Jews transcends logic itself. I love being helpful to all kinds of Jews, not because I find them to be blessed, or superior to other people, but because I feel a distinct emotional attachment to them. This love I feel may be akin to faith itself. I feel deeply Jewish, although, paradoxically, I cannot accept the Jewish theological tradition.

# 3

# THE WISE GUY OF
# FORTY-SEVENTH STREET

ITH BETTING AN EVERYDAY ACTIVITY THROUGH-
out his youth, my father became a gambler of some
repute as an adult. His friends and his business activities, along with his gambling, drew the attention
of various state and federal authorities. That certainly was not
the norm for the fathers of my friends, but little about my father was ever ordinary. Through most of his life, he rarely used
a checkbook. He paid for everything with cash. (My own
propensity to carry a lot of cash undoubtedly comes from him.)
He did not keep business records nor seriously prepare a tax return until the federal government finally discovered this over-
sight. I am sure he had no appreciation of the merits of the
income tax system; his limited education may have restricted
such understanding. Thus, not until his later years did he even
bother to get professional help in calculating his tax returns—
and then, only with disdain.

He lived in Manhattan, sometimes in the Greystone Hotel
on the Upper West Side and then in an apartment on East End
Avenue. Irregularly, he had women friends, although he usually lived alone. He tended to be a bit of a loner, yet, in his
broad social milieu, my father was very comfortable. He had
the ability to mix with a range of people, including those in

high society. He would often introduce me to people in the Social Register, particularly women whom he had met while gambling or in his extensive nightlife. He was an uninhibited show-off on the dance floor, and he possessed a robust, earthy charm.

He knew Meyer Lansky, the Jewish mobster, and right up until the time of my father's death, he remained close to Lansky's partner, Jimmy Aiello—"Jimmy Blue Eyes," as his friends called him. I met Jimmy on several occasions; he and my father saw each other at least a couple of times a year. When they got together in New York, they often ate at Patsy's, an Italian restaurant on the West Side that was frequented by Frank Sinatra and other celebrities. Jimmy was, and is, an exceptionally charming man who has a wonderful gift for gab. He appeared to me like a cherubic grandfather. In their dinners at Patsy's, my father and Jimmy talked with animated enthusiasm about the good old days. They shared a genuine affection and camaraderie when reliving past adventures, particularly gambling tales. While I sometimes caught names that I knew to be notorious, they generally avoided discussing any juicy stuff in front of me. I was, after all, a kid whom my father made sure to protect.

Plenty of other shady characters were in my father's circle. When Joey Anastasia, another acquaintance, was shot in the barbershop of the Park Sheraton Hotel, the police picked up my father for questioning. The two of them had apparently been out gambling together the night before Anastasia was killed. But I never saw this side of my father's life. He was always careful to exclude me from most of the activities about which he felt uncomfortable.

During World War II, when the federal government started buying gold at a premium price from citizens for the war effort, my father saw his chance to make some good money. He offered to buy jewelry and other gold objects from people for cash. Then he melted the pieces down and sold the gold to the government. This opportunity ultimately led him to his career.

Later, my father would tell me stories about the difficulties of his youthful period—how hard it was to "make a living." He described walking up and down the stairs of tenements in Harlem and upper Manhattan, buying old gold bracelets, rings, pins, diamonds, or whatever, from whoever would sell them to him, and never asking about the source. He had a knife scar on one leg—a legacy from those gold-buying days. When I was a child, he would point to that scar (it was near his knee) and tell me how he had been attacked on a rooftop in Harlem by someone who tried to rob him. He implied, and I distinctly recall the relish with which he recounted this part of the story, that the robber's fate had been far worse than his.

My father's gold-buying during the war became the defining opportunity of his life and led him into the jewelry business. He became a fixture on Forty-Seventh Street, in the "Diamond District" of Manhattan, where cash was often the primary medium of exchange. As a cash buyer, he was courageous and often foolhardy. From his quick and abrupt judgments, he both benefited and suffered. Everybody in the jewelry district knew him because he was such a distinctive character. He was big and burly and, perhaps because of a constant hearing problem, he spoke with a vigorous pitch. He bought and sold with all sorts of people. I even heard him referred to as the "jeweler to the mob," but this certainly was not his everyday business.

In his commercial dealings, which mostly were with other Jews, my father felt mixed and sometimes negative emotions. Like any ethnic group, Jews have their good and bad people. My father, like some non-Orthodox Jews, was prone to tar the Orthodox, in particular, with the brush of dishonesty and less-than-moral behavior. Perhaps he held them to a higher standard because of their more fervent observance of Jewish law. In moments of anger, he was known to say that the best people died in the Holocaust. He claimed that many survived only because they had made unhappy compromises or had profanely collaborated.

He once told me a story that I still find searing. He was dealing with two Orthodox jewelers and had offered them a piece of jewelry. They took the piece to sell. A few days later, apparently unsuccessful, they returned it to him. He quickly discovered that they had switched the main diamond, replacing it with a gem of much lesser quality. He was livid and intended to get revenge. He waited for some period (revenge is a dish best served cold) and then called to offer them another piece of jewelry he was sure they would like to see. He invited them to his apartment and, when they arrived, he took out a revolver and put it to their heads. He had them both go down on their knees and threatened to pull the trigger. He shouted at them for their dishonesty and stupidity in cheating him by switching the stone. They immediately confessed. They were shaking, afraid for their lives, as my father verbally abused them. Then they started to cry and opened their shirtsleeves, revealing the numbers that had been tattooed on them in the concentration camps. When my father saw the tattoos, the impact was jarring. He stopped, paced around while he decided what to do, and then disdainfully threw them out the door.

My father had his own code of ethics. It was singularly important to him, and he periodically lectured me on its content. Every father tries to instill a set of values in his offspring. My father, despite his questionable lifestyle, was no different. His actions revolved around his concepts of "honest" and "honorable." As he defined them, "honest" people paid their taxes but had no qualms about cutting every corner and using legal gimmicks to skim their payments whenever possible. Being "law abiding" was not necessarily related to being ethical. He knew far too many politicians who paraded their honesty at the same time that they feathered their nests. It was his way of pointing to the hypocrisy of bourgeois values, which he despised. "Honorable" people were those who had the resolute ability to live up to their personal commitments, no matter how difficult. The sine qua non of "honorable" people was loyalty to their friends, even under great stress. My father had a pristine reputation for integrity in his world. He took pride in being honorable, but his code was of the streets.

As a result of this code, my father always honored his commitments, regardless of the financial results. Once, in the early 1960s, my father went to London on a gambling trip. There he met a recent immigrant from Israel, Shlomo Moussaieff, a jeweler who was originally of Bukharan (Russian) descent. Shlomo had married in Israel, recently moved to London, and was starting a new business life after all sorts of financial difficulties. My father took an immediate liking to Shlomo and his wife and instinctively decided that he could trust them. Thus, before he left England, he made Shlomo an offer that could help him get back on his feet. My father left in Shlomo's possession a very valuable piece of jewelry that had once belonged to the royal family of King Farouk of Egypt. He told Shlomo that he wanted to sell it for a certain minimum price. Any amount realized above that price, he and his new friend were to share equally.

Several months later, my father returned to London. Shlomo, despite extensive efforts, had failed to sell the piece. My father took the jewelry back and, as far as Shlomo was concerned, that was the end of it. He was, nevertheless, grateful for the opportunity, and the implicit trust my father had placed in him. Several months passed and my father once again returned to London and located his new friend. Upon seeing him, my father took out a wad of cash and handed Shlomo, to his utter amazement, $25,000. My father said that he had been fortunate enough to sell the piece for a good price in the United States. They had remained partners, as far as my father was concerned, and this was his friend's share of the profits. This scenario was clearly not common practice, particularly in the jewelry business. Shlomo Moussaieff is now world-renowned as a dealer in important precious jewels, particularly with Middle Eastern clientele. He has sold some of the greatest stones that have come to the market in the last quarter of the twentieth century. He and his family have told me many times that they attribute his first success to the kindness of my father and the money he made with him.

My father and Shlomo had a lasting friendship. Often, years later, when my father visited London, he would call his friend and deposit wads of cash with him, sometimes as much as $50,000. This was my father's way of checking his predilection for squandering money on gambling. Much to Shlomo's dismay, however, my father would often call him in the middle of the night and demand, "I need my money now!" Shlomo always refused, thereby ending my father's gambling for the night. Days later, when his gambling passion had cooled, my father would thank Shlomo for having the good sense to deny his request.

∞

To me, my father was larger than life and, as a child, I idolized him. I remember once bragging to a friend that my father had played in the baseball minor leagues. He had told me this, but it was a total fabrication. My father also told me he had been in the army during World War II. Later, I discovered that also was untrue. But some elements of my father's

life I *knew* were real because, in my teenage years, he included me irregularly in some of his nighttime activities. In
the 1950s, he sometimes took me to the Copacabana, a chic
nightclub on the East Side of Manhattan, frequented by so-
cialites, celebrities, and wise guys. He was well known there
and was treated like royalty. The bouncers and doormen
greeted my father by name: "Red," or "Red McGee" because
he looked Irish, or "Reuta" in Yiddish. Given his propensity
for dispensing wads of cash, he was widely welcomed and
shown to the best table.

Frequently, there were Jewish comedians on stage, such as
Joey Lewis and Joe E. Brown, and they often acknowledged
my father's presence during their acts. He invariably ordered
Dom Perignon because he believed it to be the best champagne. Moreover, everyone knew it was the most expensive
champagne on the menu. He was well known among the
nightclub's clientele and shady-looking characters. Some sent
bottles of champagne (again, Dom Perignon) from their tables
or joined us at ours. In retrospect, the nightclub scene was
right out of the movie *Goodfellas*. In contrast to Bensonhurst,
this glamour awed me and I mostly enjoyed these irregular
outings. My father was a big shot there, and I had a sense of
pride in him.

I am still not sure which of my father's activities were
myth and which were fact. His stories about pre-Castro Cuba
and his ownership interest in casinos there, about winning
and losing bets of mind-boggling magnitude, about his foibles
with women—all these were beyond a child's, and even a
teenager's, ability to comprehend. He was often the center of
attention, adored by his friends (including his girlfriends),
and extraordinarily free with cash. He often gave me one or
two $100 bills when I saw him during my teenage years.
What a contrast to the man whom my mother had known
only 10 or so years before—the man who often failed to come

up with his court-determined $50 per month for child support. In the years since I was a baby, my father's financial circumstances had improved.

∽

In 1953, my father sometimes gambled with a Wall Street broker who worked at Reynolds Securities. Somehow, he persuaded my father to purchase shares in two companies about which my father knew nothing. Indeed, he was ignorant about financial markets in general. These stock purchases occurred just before my Bar Mitzvah and, almost as an afterthought, my father gave me the shares as a gift for my passage into manhood. I received 100 shares of Penn Dixie Cement and 100 shares of Columbia Gas System, the first shares of stock I ever owned. I still remember that Penn Dixie was selling at $37 a share and Columbia Gas was selling at $16. Together, they were worth over $5,000, an enormous amount of money for a 13-year-old. The gift was extraordinary, almost beyond my grasp in a world where Bar Mitzvah gifts usually ranged from $5 to $20 or consisted of a U.S. Savings Bond with a value of $25 or $50 only after many years. My father gave me these shares without fanfare, and I was not easily able to express gratitude—certainly not in proportion to this gift. No one around me knew a thing about stocks or the stock market. It would be up to me to find out.

This gift galvanized me. I was captivated not just because the shares were worth more money than I had ever known, but also because there was something enticing about their value and how it fluctuated. I could go to sleep at night with the certificates safely stashed in my dresser drawer, and somehow, when I woke up the next morning, their value had changed. If Penn Dixie went up $1, that was a $100 gain—a major change in my financial net worth, given the fact that my allowance was about $4 a week.

Two years later, when I was 15 years old, my mother, through great effort, managed to get me my first summer job as a storeroom worker at a local grocery. Lifting and moving cartons of canned goods was backbreaking work, and I hated it. Over the course of the summer, I earned a little more than $100. Making $100 overnight on my stock certificates clearly was preferable.

Fascination with these shares inevitably led to an intense interest in the stock market. I did everything I could to learn about stocks and the market. I found the sections of the newspapers that covered stocks, and I figured out what the mysterious abbreviations and symbols stood for. I eventually started getting and reading two or three editions of the *New York World Telegraph & Sun* to see the intraday price changes. The paper had a noon, two o'clock, and closing edition each day.

I soon learned that a few brokerage houses had offices in downtown Brooklyn. Before long, I was skipping stickball games to monitor the day's action in the stock market. I must admit that no other aspect of my teenage life could compete with the thrill I felt when the final schoolbell rang and I caught the subway to the business section of downtown Brooklyn. I would get off at DeKalb Avenue and head straight to the brokerage office of Bache & Company.

To me, Bache & Company represented an entirely new world in all its color, pace, and intensity. As soon as I walked in, I was caught up in the adrenaline flow of dozens of men, many with cigars dangling from their mouths, who darted from desk to desk, placed trades, and watched the ticker tape's exotic symbols go by. I sat in the seats provided for visitors, and I watched the brokers, known as "customers' men," in awe. The stench of the cigars, the blur of men gesticulating on phones—all of it overloaded my senses. This was no country club; it was the rough-and-tumble of Wall Street, with all the opportunistic commotion one would expect. Every broker had a story to tell,

41

a stock to push, a commission to generate. Men whispered tips and merger rumors. Many spoke of "sure things," which, we have long ago learned, do not exist. They also whispered other bits of the largely ineffective gibberish to be expected in such an environment. They were all there with only one purpose: to make as much money as they could between the opening bell and the closing bell.

I was just a kid, so most of the brokers ignored me, but, after a while, a few of them began to notice that I was there almost every day. Occasionally, they would acknowledge my presence with a nod. I liked watching my stocks go by on the ticker tape. I learned their symbols and I charted the progress of companies I was interested in. The noise of the ticker only exacerbated the delirium of the environment. Not only did you see the ticker, you heard it too. The greater the activity in the market, the more rapid the sound of the ticker. There was, then, a certain music to the market, and when its tempo increased it became that much more exciting.

In my spare time, I began to read annual reports and Standard & Poor's sheets, which gave brief summary descriptions of each company. These became particularly fascinating because they gave me an effective snapshot of complex enterprises. My first taste of American capitalism filled my young teenage mind with breathtaking imagery. At this point in my life, a subway ride to Manhattan remained a major adventure; yet I could learn about, and potentially own shares in, companies that actually existed in far-off places like Ohio, California, and Indiana. Moreover, those shares represented real assets–tangible things such as quarries, cement-making plants, trucks, and more. The stock market opened up to me a whole new world to explore.

I soon graduated from the DeKalb Avenue brokerage office of Bache & Company and moved on to Manhattan. In those days, Merrill, Lynch, Pierce, Fenner and Smith had an educational office in Grand Central Station. I went there and proudly opened up my first brokerage account (with my mother as custodian). There, even more information was available to the public. The office had a computer—one that would certainly be considered primitive today. Nonetheless, it provided up-to-date information on various companies. To me, it was the height of technological sophistication. I would go there whenever I could, read research material on the stocks I was interested in, and bring home gobs of paper. Merrill Lynch, like most other brokerage firms, produced vast amounts of research on individual stocks, as well as broad industry coverage. In that optimistic period, a range of themes dominated the brokerage business. One theme was: Invest in America's Future. I did. I ended up buying a number of the stocks that I read about.

Like most novices, I was a painfully inept investor in those early days. In the stock market, almost everyone pays a price, sometimes substantial for even an introductory education. I had not yet learned what prudence or caution meant nor had "risk" entered my vocabulary. As a result, I fell for a number of scams. I eagerly sent away for most of the free investment advisory reports I saw advertised in the paper. In the end, some of those free reports cost me a great deal of what little money I had to invest.

I have one particular memory of buying shares in Swan-Finch Oil. I had seen an advertisement for a free report, and I sent for it. The report extolled the virtues of this unique investment opportunity, so I called the broker who had written it. He totally entranced me with his pitch. I thought I had found a really great opportunity. It was, of course, a fraud, run from what were then called "bucket shops": securities firms that employed salespeople who dealt in over-the-counter stocks of dubious value, and promoted or "pushed" them to unwary, unsophisticated individuals like me. I remember buying several hundred shares from this broker, and then the price went down. I finagled my mother into speaking to the broker. He pitched her as well. She ended up *buying* shares. As the stock went down further, he persuaded us to buy more. This naturally only compounded our mistake because the stock ended up being worthless. If one were to measure my performance as a high-school investor, it would be a sorry tale. While the total losses could be measured in relatively few thousands of dollars, they seemed horrific at the time. Even back then, I did not suffer losses lightly. The alternative of working in a grocery store again loomed large. Moreover, the fact that my hard-working mother had lost even a penny further enraged me. That, I swore, would never happen again.

Whatever the results, my interest in the market was so intense that it dwarfed any other pursuits. I knew I wanted to work on Wall Street and, once I had made up my mind, I never thought about any other career. It was not work, it was joy. I had come to love the risk taking associated with trading, and the rush that comes when the risk pays off. Watching the "moving parts" of being right and being rewarded was a speculative joy. I have no doubt that I inherited this love of the rush from my father, who lived his life taking risks and pushing boundaries. Psychologically, emotionally, and perhaps even intellectually, gambling and the manner in which I then invested may not have been importantly different.

For much of my life, however, I have been comforted by the knowledge that to be successful in the stock market requires a substantial education, in terms of both information and experience. The stock market, unlike most games of chance, is not random. As the cliché states, it is always "better to be lucky than smart," but one should never make a bet on a stock and hope that one will be lucky. Developing expertise does result in better performance. But the speculative joy, the joy derived from being right and being rewarded, may well be similar to the rush felt by a winning gambler. My good fortune in seeking that joy in the stock market, rather than in horse racing or crap games, may have been merely due to my place in time rather than my own wisdom. My father's gift of those two stocks played as significant a role in the shaping of my life as anything else that happened to me before or after.

My father was not around much, and he certainly was not dependable for fulfilling a traditional parental role, but every once in a while he would do something—make a gesture, offer a nudge, or, in this case, give me a gift—that would have repercussions well beyond anything I could have imagined. I regret not appreciating him more.

As a result, I probably looked elsewhere for a more traditional father figure. I remember a man my mother dated for a time—Ben Mackover, whom I adored. I loved his warmth and his kindness. For a period of several years, before my Bar Mitzvah, I would see him with my mother once or twice a week. He had become a substitute father figure for me. At my Bar Mitzvah, the very event at which my father gave me the shares of stock that changed my life, it was Ben, not my father, to whom I made a gesture showing that closeness. The traditional gift of the day for a Bar Mitzvah boy was a white envelope with cash. Before long, my pockets spilled over with cash-filled white envelopes. Eventually, I needed someone to help me hold them. I asked Ben, not my father, to hold on to the envelopes. I did this, quite simply, because I felt *closer* to Ben than to my father.

When Ben took my mother and me to Nathan's, at Coney Island, that outing was one of the highlights of my week. I vividly remember standing near the counter at Nathan's and inhaling the salty smell of the Atlantic Ocean as it washed over the sand beyond the boardwalk. I loved Nathan's hamburgers and French fries; then and now, those are the best French fries I have ever had. Sometimes I even had fried shrimp, which was a real treat. Nathan's was, and is, world-famous for its hot dogs, but I preferred its hamburgers and French fries. At home, we were very careful with our spending money; even going to Nathan's was a special treat. I always associated Ben with this treat, and wished that he and my mother would marry. After we finished eating, if we had time, we went for a walk. Ben and my mother strolled along the wide wooden boardwalk, and I stayed nearby on the beach.

Outings like our trips to Nathan's helped me develop a close relationship with Ben, a confirmed bachelor who never married my mother. That he enjoyed being around me meant a lot. So, on the day of my Bar Mitzvah, it seemed natural to hand the cash-filled envelopes to Ben instead of my father. But later, after the Bar Mitzvah was over, my mother pointed out that my father was watching as I handed the envelopes to Ben. He was embarrassed and, no doubt, his feelings were hurt. In hindsight, I felt bad that I had slighted him, but there was nothing I could do to rectify the situation. Awkward discomfort often marked my relationship with my father.

Many years later, when I was an adult, I received a phone call one day from a man named Ben Mackover. I picked up the phone and the person sounded old and feeble. He told me he had seen my name in the newspaper and wondered if I was the Michael Steinhardt whom he had known as a child. I told him I was. We reminisced about those trips to Nathan's. He asked about my mother. We had a good chat, and I enjoyed reliving a memory or two with him. I could almost smell the salty ocean air and taste those delicious hamburgers and French fries. That was the last time I ever heard from Ben.

⚭

There was another element that further strained my complicated relationship with my father. Not only was he unreliable and seemingly capricious, he also had a temper. His anger could appear in a flash and at the most inopportune times. His temper sometimes got in the way of our enjoying our time together and never more so than when he was gambling.

For example, I remember occasionally going to Giants games with my father. I always loved the Giants, even though this made me different from most of my friends who rooted for the Dodgers. I did not care. I may even have enjoyed my distinction and the arguments that ensued.

I knew every player on the roster: his history, his batting average, the full range of his statistics. In 1951, I cried when Bobby Thomson hit "the shot heard 'round the world." I will never forget sitting in the living room of our apartment in Brooklyn and listening as Russ Hodges, the radio announcer, shouted: "The Giants win the pennant! The Giants win the pennant!"

Another memory associated with the Giants is not so pleasant. One Sunday, when I was 11 years old, my father took me to see the Giants play the Cincinnati Reds at the Polo Grounds. Usually, my mother took me to games, but never as many as I would have liked. Mostly, I listened to games on the radio. When we could finally afford to buy a television, I watched the games.

I was thrilled to be at the Polo Grounds for a rare outing with my father. I did not pay much attention to him when he mentioned, during the first inning, in an off-the-cuff sort of way, that he was rooting for the Reds. I am not sure why the comment did not make an impression on me, since it was strange that he was not rooting for our home team. Maybe it was simply because he said it under his breath, as though it were not important.

The game turned out to be exciting. The score was close all the way through. The Reds were ahead in the eighth inning, 4 to 2. Then the Giants got two men on base with Don Mueller up at the plate. A relatively undistinguished player, Mueller was not a home-run hitter. An average lefty, he did have the home-field advantage of the Polo Grounds' short right field. On the second pitch, he hit a high pop that just made it into the lower deck—another cheap Polo Grounds home run. I could not believe it! As Mueller's hit cleared the wall, I jumped up with the unrestrained enthusiasm of a kid. The Giants were now ahead, 5 to 4. It was the kind of storybook, come-from-behind moment that baseball fantasies are made of. Moreover, it was my team that had done it.

While Mueller rounded the bases, it seemed the only person *not* celebrating was seated next to me. My father was silent. Indeed, when I looked at him more closely, I could tell he was not happy at all. He was sitting in his seat, agitated and miserable. I did not know what to make of him. I remembered he had said he was pulling for Cincinnati, but I could not figure out why he was taking Mueller's home run so badly. When the Reds did not score in the ninth, the crowd went wild, but my father began to glare at me even more intensely. As I joined the cheering, my father suddenly stood up and punched me in the shoulder. Not playfully; hard, menacingly. I was shocked. He had never hit me like this, and I did not know what to do.

"How can you be so stupid?" my father yelled. "Do you think Don Mueller is going to pay your bills? Do you think the Giants are going to pay for your college education? You know, you are a fool. I mean, do you have any idea how much money I just lost on this game?"

Nothing he said really sank in. I was so stunned by the fact that he had hit me, I started to cry. This only made him angrier. To this day, I will never forget my father's rage at the game that afternoon. My relationship with my father was never simple.

# 4

# THE IVY LEAGUE, THE ARMY, AND THE STREET

ECAUSE OF MY ACCELERATED PROGRAM IN junior high school, I was only 16 during my high school senior year, when I was contemplating college. I decided on the Bernard Baruch Business School in Manhattan, which was part of the City College of New York. This was the likely choice for me since it was tuition-free for New Yorkers with a certain grade average. I would have to pay only for my books and supplies. Almost all the college kids I knew from Bensonhurst went through the City University system. But once again, my father showed up unexpectedly, altered my plans, and changed my life.

One Sunday, my father invited me to dinner at one of his favorite restaurants, the Sacred Cow Steakhouse on West Seventy-second Street in Manhattan. During dinner, he asked me what college I planned to attend. He had never finished high school, so I had assumed he would be indifferent to my choice. I told him I had already been accepted at Bernard Baruch.

"It's the right place for me because it's a business school," I said, "and I'm interested in the stock market. Anyway, since I have a high enough grade point average, I can go there basically for free."

My father looked at me. "That ain't the place you want to be," he said flatly. He ate a bite of his steak. "There's a school in Philadelphia, I know it's a business school, where I see a lot of wealthy Jewish boys have graduated."

"How do you know?" I said.

"I see their wedding announcements in the Sunday *New York Times* Society Section."

He put down his fork and knife and spoke to me as if he were negotiating a deal.

"Try to get in there," he said. "You get in, and I'll pay for it."

I did not understand why he was telling me to do this. "But I think all the deadlines have passed."

"So you'll be early for next year. Just apply."

The school, of course, was the Wharton School at the University of Pennsylvania. At that time, I, unlike many of my peers, was not sensitive to the relative prestige of a school like Penn. The world of the Ivy League—the gilded world of an elite with its own dress code and rules of conduct—was foreign to me. Socially, I had been rather slow growing up. I had not dated in high school. I rarely had anything to do with girls. I knew little of social graces; I guess I was a nerd. After school, whenever I was free, I would hang out with the guys. We still played stickball and touch football, if I was not doing something related to the market.

Despite my lack of sophistication, I took my father's advice and, at the last minute, applied to Wharton. Much to my surprise, they accepted me. When I called my father to tell him, he did not seem surprised or even excited. He just reiterated that I should go there and he would pay.

In retrospect, I can see that one of the reasons my mother wanted me to maintain a relationship with my father was her understanding that someday he might be able to help me, and he *would* help if he could. Throughout my youth, I was not innately responsive to my father. Not just because he could be

awful, as he was that day at the Giants–Reds game, but because I blamed him for the breakup of my parents' marriage,
which led to my mother's having a hard life and to my not
having a two-parent home. I felt anxious whenever I called
my father or when I heard he was on the phone, waiting to
talk to me. Given his range of moods, I never knew what to
expect, and I often had reason to fear his temper. I struggled
with what to call him. Even in periods when I felt genuine affection, I could not quite call him "Dad." When I wrote letters to him, they started with "Dear Dad," but in personal
conversation those words did not feel right. This awkward-
ness probably bothered him as much as it did me. Still, my
mother encouraged me not to cut him out of my life, and she
was right.

I remember being nervous when my father did show up. I
was wary of him. Yet, I wanted to spend time with him, and I
hoped our time together would fit some ideal father-son
image I held. On balance, I was glad to see him, despite his
dark side. His mood changes could be rapid and, at times,
scary. Even so, I dealt with him and he had a tremendous effect on my life if for no other reason than because he gave me
those stocks for my Bar Mitzvah and then afforded me the
chance to go to Wharton.

My mother raised me, and, as a single parent, she alone
bore the tribulations of my growing up. She was my most stal-
wart companion throughout childhood and adolescence. In
every way, she devoted her life to me, whether through putting food on the table or taking me to ball games or the zoo.
She worked hard—she was never really secure—and she must
have been very lonely. I cannot exaggerate my mother's self-
less devotion. It is one of life's ironies that, as a child, I had little but felt totally secure—perhaps more so than when I
became an affluent adult. My mother did not judge me and
did not pressure me about school; she gave me unconditional

love. Because my mother's love protected me, I felt at home with my friends, my family, and my neighborhood. I never had a sense of doing without. I did not feel a desire for upward mobility, nor did I feel driven to escape my origins. I know now that money was scarce, but whatever was not taken care of just did not matter. My father provided an opportunity to get ahead in life by offering to pay for my college tuition, but it was my mother who had prepared me to take it.

∞

When I arrived at the University of Pennsylvania in the fall of 1957, I was an immature 16-year-old Jewish kid from Brooklyn. Penn exposed me to a culture entirely different from the one I had grown up in. The clothing the students wore struck me first. I did not dress like my classmates. Many of them had grown up rich; many had attended prep schools. They seemed to have their own dress code. They had the right button-down shirts. They knew where to buy their jackets. They wore their sweaters in just the right way, sometimes hung over their shoulders, with the sleeves tied in front. I was never conscious of how people dressed in Bensonhurst. But this was the Ivy League and there I was at Penn—a socially backward kid who was in love with the stock market but did not know the difference between a sports jacket and a suit coat.

My first roommate was a fellow named David Irving. The son of a navy captain, he also came from a different world. He was conservative, straight-laced, and Christian. He was a person of character and we got along well, though it took me a while to become relaxed in our friendship. Ultimately, most of the friends I made at Penn were Jewish; the school had a relatively large Jewish population. There were Jewish fraternities of varying status, but I, being socially backward, was not accepted, though I did participate in rushing. I ate my dinners at Hillel, the Jewish campus organization, not because it was kosher but because it offered an easy entry into campus social life. I met one of my lifelong friends, Harry Freund, at Hillel.

Our friendship began instantaneously. Harry came to Penn from an upper-middle-class decidedly Jewish family in Manhattan. He had gone to an Orthodox day school. His mother, who had been president of Hadassah for a considerable period, was prominent among Jewish philanthropic leaders. Harry had grown up in an isolated Jewish world so attending Penn, with its ethnic diversity, was an experience as new to him as it was to me. When studying academic subjects of any sort, Harry could not help but use the Talmudic method of saying, or at times sing-songing aloud, whatever he wanted to memorize, to the great annoyance of his neighbors. Because he had a Jewish interpretation for everything, I would sometimes accuse him of having a Jewish monomania. At Penn, Harry's focus was so intently Jewish that I, in part, credit my own Jewish identity to my friendship with him. I even made a bet with him that he would someday make *aliyah* (immigrate to Israel). I am still waiting to collect; the only *aliyah* I have seen has been from Westchester back to Manhattan.

Yet, some of the classes I took, and the intellectual ferment of a college campus, again encouraged me to question the tradition I had been taught in my youth. Despite my growing theological doubts, every day, from my Bar Mitzvah at age 13 to my entry into college at age 16, I had put on tefillin and said morning prayers. Starting the day with this five-minute ritual somehow made me feel good and at peace with myself. Back then, the inconsistency of these prayers and my atheism did not bother me.

At Penn, however, I was exposed to history, philosophy, and science—the fundamentals of a liberal secular education. I began to further question religion. I revisited my doubts about the existence of God. Like so many people, I struggled with

the question of evil. If there is a God and that God is omnis-
cient and omnipotent, how could He allow pain and suffering,
particularly of the innocent, to exist in the world? Are the theological responses—that God's ways are generally beyond com-
prehension—the best we can muster? That line did not satisfy
me, nor did the other usually amorphous theisms that I tasted.
So, almost unconsciously, I returned to my childhood doubts
and became, to my mother's dismay, a self-avowed atheist. I
knew my mother's sensitivities and beliefs, but being an intellectual purist took priority. I remember one Yom Kippur during college when I provoked my mother, her brother's family,
and some cousins, by eating in front of them as they fasted. In
the past, I had enjoyed debating theological issues with my relatives, but now when I conspicuously munched away, there
were only silent stares. For me, it was an empty victory.

After I left for college, my mother moved into a smaller
apartment in Bensonhurst, on West Seventh Street between
Bay Parkway and Avenue O. I felt good occasionally going
home on weekends wearing my red-and-blue Penn jacket and
seeing my neighborhood friends. This was still the era when
boys went to college in greater numbers than girls. Some of
my classmates did not go at all. Many of the girls were hoping
to marry right after high school. Of my high school classmates
who did go to college, most had not left New York. They attended the city schools or other schools in the New York area.
I was an exception, thanks to my father.

Because my mother had no money and I was not confident
that my father would pay my college bills all the way through,
I decided to condense my course-load and graduate in three
years instead of four. I accomplished this by taking an extra full
load of credits in my second and third years, and attending two
summer sessions at New York University. On a three-year
plan, however, I could not fit in all the prerequisites for a major
in finance, which demanded a traditional four-year span.

Therefore, I chose to major in sociology because it afforded many single courses that did not demand prerequisites. I started out a very good student and made the Dean's List during my first year at Penn, but, from the second year on, I loaded myself down with so many extra classes that my grades were just low enough to keep me off the Dean's List.

The most valuable class I took at Penn, the one that had the most influence on my thinking, was an advanced course called Philosophy of Statistics, taught by Dr. Francis Brown. I had always been comfortable with numbers and statistics, but this course offered a framework for understanding probabilities better, in both familiar and remote applications. In class, we learned how to frame problems quantitatively so as to arrive at unexpected probability distributions, and how to develop some formulas where none seemed possible. This study of statistics, combined with my major in sociology, was a superb combination for a career in the stock market. Mastering statistics helped me apply probability theory with great comfort, and the sociology exposed me to ways of thinking about human behavior with a mathematical overview.

With this background, I could interpret a range of quantitative issues with sufficient numeric impact to gain a confidence not easily achieved otherwise. Even limited quantification made me comfortable with analyzing areas about which, at best, I had partial knowledge. Thus years later, this made me better equipped to deal with decision making on a multitude of issues with incomplete data that define the reality of the investment process involved. Probability analysis of some sort is a part of every investment calculation. I learned this discipline early and, over time, would apply it well.

∞

During my time at Penn, my father was arrested. For years, the FBI had followed him, as they did many of his gambling friends and associates. In 1958, Frank Hogan, the District Attorney of Manhattan, arrested my father and announced publicly that he had apprehended the biggest jewel fence in America, Sol Frank Steinhardt. I did not know how to react. I felt shame, especially because of the media attention. People knew he was my father. He vigorously protested his innocence, and I believed him. Perhaps because of the irregular nature of our relationship, there had always been a distance between us, but the sense that he was being assaulted unfairly made me feel closer to him.

The trial, filled with theatrics, lasted more than six weeks and received unusual media focus. All sorts of improbable things occurred. At one point, Burton Roberts, the Assistant District Attorney who was trying the case, walked over to the jury box during a lull in the proceedings, pointed to somebody sitting in the courtroom, and said, "See that guy there? He's a friend of the defendant and he's a killer!" He paused before he grabbed his crotch and said, "And I don't mean this kind of killer either." In those days, "killer" was a Yiddish euphemism for hernia.

To me, the proceedings had an otherworldly quality. On the days I attended the trial, my father and his attorney appeared to be in a good mood, along with everyone else in the courtroom. It resembled a low-budget circus, with witnesses brought from prison, ex-convicts, strange women, and other sleazy bystanders performing in various rings. I remember times when I wanted to deny that my father and I were related, but I had to accept the reality of who and what my father was.

Ultimately, *People v. Steinhardt* became a classic case of misplaced prosecutorial zeal and misconduct. It was a sad reflection on our system of justice. My father was found guilty on two felony counts and sentenced to prison. For each count, he received 5 to 10 years, to be served consecutively, not concurrently. It was the longest sentence he could have been given as a first-time offender. He lost his first appeal, four to one. Had all five judges found against him, the appeal process would have ended. But my father was lucky. That one judge kept his case alive.

Through a friend and cousin of mine, Phil Kosowsky, I hired a lawyer who taught at Brooklyn Law School. He won a second appeal for my father, largely on the basis of the District Attorney's misconduct. Instead of moving for a new trial, the court agreed to release my father on the basis of time served (almost two years), if my father accepted the felony charge. He did.

His prison experience was a story unto itself. He started his sentence at Sing Sing, in Westchester County, before being transferred to Dannemora, a maximum security prison in the middle of nowhere, in upstate New York. The transfer was a punishment for the supposed "favors" my father was receiving at Sing Sing. It was quite an ordeal to get up there, and seeing my father was no pleasure either. He seethed, claiming that his own lawyer had framed him and that the entire system was corrupt, starting with the prosecutor's office. In prison, his intensity led him to ruin his teeth by grinding them incessantly. He had them all recapped as soon as he got out.

At the time, I believed, totally, in my father's innocence. He told me he was innocent. He pleaded "Not guilty." He described the terrible injustice he felt was being done to him, and I believed him. Over time, I have come to have a different opinion. Whether he was guilty or not in this particular instance, he had certainly engaged in purchasing stolen jewelry at various times in his life. However, it is one thing to have engaged in such an activity; it is another to be convicted unfairly in a court of law. He did engage in illegal activities, but they seemed minor compared with the shoddiness and corruption of the judicial system during his trial. The experience led me to be far more cynical than I would have liked to be about this domain. Burton Roberts, the prosecuting ADA, eventually became a judge and was rumored to be the model for the judge in Tom Wolfe's bestseller, *Bonfire of the Vanities*.

∞

In 1960, after I had graduated from Wharton and headed to New York to look for a job on Wall Street, I was concerned that potential employers might identify me as the son of Sol Frank Steinhardt. Fortunately, no one did. Instead, I had other, more immediate, problems. At age 19, I was unsophisticated. In fact, because I did not have any connections and could not find any shortcuts, I went through an impersonal and unpleasant process: "pounding the pavement" and applying for jobs through employment agencies. I had graduated a year ahead of my friends, which meant I was job-hunting alone, and I had majored in sociology, not the best field of study for an ideal candidacy on Wall Street. After stirring no interest at a number of Wall Street firms, I began applying to insurance companies. Several interviewers asked me, "Steinhardt—is that a German name?" I began to feel self-consciously Jewish, whatever the intent of the question.

Finally, at Calvin Bullock, a traditional white-shoe mutual fund organization, I sparked some interest in the person interviewing me and was given the chance to meet with the head of the research department. The meeting went well, and I was offered a $75-a-week job as a statistical assistant doing basic research. Needless to say, I accepted the job at once.

I had not taken any investment courses at Wharton, and, despite my teenage apprenticeship in the market, I was unfamiliar with how Wall Street really worked. At Calvin Bullock, I learned a good deal about the structure of the investment management business. Actually, I was exposed to the height of professionalism there. Decisions were based on careful scrutiny of balance sheets, income statements, and annual reports.

Meetings with company management and consultations with analysts followed. Only after serious discussions among the senior investment executives of the firm was there a recommendation. This rigorous tiered process had its own structure, its own constraints, and its own life. It was vastly different from anything I had known or experienced earlier.

I spent my days generating macrostatistical research for our weekly department meetings. Before long, I was doing individual company analysis too. I felt like a kid in a candy store. I was surrounded by research reports, industry manuals, and library files—all filled with the kinds of information that had fascinated me for years. It was an exciting time for me. I had managed to transfer my teenage avocation into a fulfilling work experience and was even improving my investing in the stock market. I loved the work. Almost every night, I was the last to leave.

I also continued my education in more traditional ways. At night, I went to New York University's Graduate Business School, which was at that time located just three blocks from Wall Street, and drew heavily upon the experienced securities professionals willing to teach a course or two. Unfortunately, I slept through a variety of interesting courses, including Henry Kaufman's course on monetary policy. I did not attend long enough to receive an MBA, although I did feel that the quality of teaching was superb.

After Wharton, "home" was my mother's new apartment in Bensonhurst. I commuted to work on the subway. Living with my mother again was initially all right, but I soon recognized the need to strike out on my own.

I called my friend from Penn, Harry Freund, and, ultimately, we roomed together at East Seventy-ninth Street, on the Upper East Side of Manhattan. We were uniquely different in style and personal characteristics. It would have been easy to persuade moviegoers that *The Odd Couple* was based on us.

Harry was conservative, careful, and personally fastidious. He was neat and meticulous in habit and appearance. I, on the other hand, was oblivious to neatness in clothes or in the various housekeeping tasks that were necessary to give our apartment a semblance of order. One time, Harry decided to experiment and *not* take out the garbage as he had regularly done. He wanted to find out how long it would be before I noticed the mess and did something about it. After two weeks, and the necessity of climbing over garbage bags to get to the front door, he finally gave up and carried out the garbage himself.

Harry was unusually sensitive to all sorts of environmental maladies. He preferred to avoid extremes of weather in general, and he constantly worried about the sun. He would walk down the street holding an open newspaper over his head, to avoid having the sun's rays on his face.

Harry also made sure to be totally immaculate all the time. Once, I was going to drive him to Ocean Parkway, in Brooklyn, to attend a party given by a girlfriend of his. Harry did not, and still does not, to this day, drive. It was a snowy day. My trusty old Plymouth convertible had been left on the street for some time and was caked all over with the combination of dirty snow and ice that is always the worst residue of a New York snowstorm. I tried to turn on the wipers, to clear the windshield, but they were completely stuck in the icy grime.

I took a towel out of the trunk while Harry, using the ever-present Wash 'n Dri towelettes he carried to groom himself, cleared the back window. I worked on the front. When I had finished, Harry was still working on the back window with two towelettes. I said, "Harry, use this," and threw him the filthy towel. Not being particularly athletic, he saw the towel coming but could not respond fast enough. The towel, with all its filth, wrapped around his face. For the rest of the trip, he did not speak to me, but from every crevice he produced more Wash 'n Dri's than I thought could be annually manufactured.

He used them all until, finally, he was sufficiently satisfied that the dirt from the towel had been completely removed.

Despite our incongruities, our living arrangement lasted for several years. Harry and I are still close friends and can share many laughs about those days. I suspect that an objective observer might conclude that I got the better end of the deal. I would have to agree.

Around this time, my father began loaning me money to start investing. Before long, I had a stock portfolio worth $200,000, a substantial sum of money for a 20-year-old in the early 1960s. But, at Calvin Bullock, the business was not based on serving customers like my father. Calvin Bullock catered to mainstream investors and sought to identify the best companies in America for long-term growth. Superior, time-sensitive, innovative money management, the ideal that was to characterize my career in investing, was not the driving force at Calvin Bullock. Instead, sustained growth through conventional research was the hallmark. It was a gentlemanly approach to solid, traditional, conservative investing. It did not include undue risk taking, at least by the common wisdom of the mutual fund world.

Sir Hugh Bullock, a tall, regal, well-spoken gentleman, ran the company. He embodied the firm and its virtues and principles, and he often spoke in the nautical metaphors that dominated the decor of the company's offices and printed material. In Sir Hugh's office, a model of an old, elaborately masted sailing ship was prominently displayed in a glass case. The company's weekly newsletter, *The Ship's Log,* often spoke of the economic environment in terms of "rough seas" and "steady courses." At Calvin Bullock, the goal was not so much to win the race as to get the ship to port with all hands safely on board.

My fondest memory of Calvin Bullock came from the company's annual black-tie dinner, the second of the two I attended. Once a year, the firm brought all of its regional mutual fund wholesalers to New York for two days and nights of conferences, banquets, and camaraderie. The main event was a dinner held on the second night–a formal affair just for executives. This entirely male event was held at one of the city's oldest clubs–one that I knew did not encourage Jewish members and may have even barred them outright.

Sir Hugh always gave the evening's final speech. At my first banquet, I listened as he talked about the firm in an enthusiastic spiel filled with the usual nautical metaphors: the captain at the helm, the rough seas rising, a star to steer by, the sound ship, the brave crew, and so on. Finally, summing up, he said, "And this is a firm of Christian gentlemen," as his eyes roamed over the room with approval, "because like attracts like." I looked around and saw that, besides me, Hugh was right. On this occasion, more than any other, I knew what it felt like to be a Jew in a Christian world.

During the next year, I continued to enjoy my job, became better at it, and got to know Sir Hugh on a more personal basis. At the second annual dinner that I attended, Sir Hugh rose and gave his speech, again offering up the firm's history in glowing nautical terms, and articulating the virtues that had brought us through the rough seas of the market. When he came to the end of his speech, he began the sentence I had heard the year before: "And this is a firm of . . ."–at that critical moment, he scanned the room, and when his eyes found mine, he paused. Finally, he said, ". . . of gentlemen, because like attracts like."

It was the highlight of my first job on Wall Street.

∞

In late 1961, my tenure at Calvin Bullock ended because of military service. Though I had not been drafted, I was subject to call-up. I chose to go for a six-month stint of active duty in the army, followed by six years' reserve duty in the National Guard.

I was 21 when, in November, I reported to Fort Dix in New Jersey. Being in the army was a life experience I can look back on with amusement, warmth, some comfortable familiarity, and a peculiar sadomasochism. I was in the best shape of my life; it was the last time I weighed 185 pounds. Some lifelong friends were first met while in uniform. Because of their unconstrained hilarity, some "uniquely army" experiences have become lifetime memories. At least, that is how I feel about it *now*. At the time, it was mostly awful. I was living in cramped quarters with strangers. I met a variety of people, most of whom were not a type I would ever again meet. One only encounters such a cross-section of society in the military.

It is a remarkable testament to America that, in two generations, the presence of the military in the lives of most people has all but disappeared. One sees more weapons and more military presence in one day in Israel than in a year in the United States. The probability that the next generation of Americans will wear a uniform seems remote. In the third quarter of the twentieth century, however, that was not the case. For me, the possibility of an active-duty call-up because of a crisis in Cuba, or the Vietnam War, was all too real.

Military training reflects a mix of fantasy and reality. One of the programs the army had created in the early 1960s for advanced infantry training bore the name "Escape and Evasion." For a full day, we were given a series of lectures and directives on these two subjects; that night, we were ordered to play war games that would show us what we would face in a wartime situation. Those in charge of our training intended this acquired knowledge about escape and evasion to help us if the enemy captured us. The army had developed this program because some American POWs performed poorly during the Korean War.

After a day of sitting in lectures and learning about the Geneva Code and the use of the compass and other field devices, my company was dropped off at dusk at a wood-line on one side of a forest. We were ordered to make our way through the forest, which was several miles wide, and get to the wood-line on the other side. Between the start and the finish, an "enemy" company (GIs pretending to be the enemy) hidden in the forest would try to capture us.

I remember heading off into the cold, wintry woods. Everybody spread out, and I was left alone. As I walked deeper into the pitch-black forest, I began to hear in the far distance what sounded like screams, blood-curdling screams. The farther I walked, the louder the screams became. I could not tell exactly where the screams were coming from, but they were chilling.

Then, suddenly, up ahead, I heard noise. I hit the ground and froze. I sensed that people were being "captured." Moments later, someone walked over to me, shined a flashlight in my face, and I was caught. Next, he put me with a group of other "prisoners." We were taken to a compound that resembled a prison camp. It had barbed wire around it and log huts inside. The terrible screaming I had heard was coming from inside one of the log huts. The "enemy" soldiers took us near that particular hut and lined us up against a wall in the main room. Soon an officer stood before us and said, "Listen, you can get out of this and go back to your barracks at any time. All you have to do is tell us something besides your name, rank, and serial number. Tell us what outfit you're from and you can leave. After all, this is just a silly war game. What are you wasting your time for, anyway?"

Naturally, we had been trained not to reveal more than our name, rank, and serial number. The "enemy" soldiers, who were mostly black NCOs, surrounded and began harassing us. They chose six of us to pick up a heavy railroad tie and carry it around over our heads. Then, in this position, a sergeant came over and kicked me, just hard enough. "All you have to do," he yelled, "is tell me your outfit." During this time, in a nearby building, the screaming continued. Finally, the sergeant took me into the hut where the screams had been coming from. "It's your turn," he said.

Inside, two guys ordered me to strip off all of my clothes. Then they grabbed me and took me to a chair that had electrodes attached to it. "Sit down," they said. They tied my hands and legs to the chair. Next, they affixed the electrodes to my naked body and started in on me again: "Tell us your outfit!" When I would not say anything, they gave a signal. A man sitting at a desk nearby turned a knob on a machine and I suddenly felt an electric current shoot through my body. The pain was astonishing. Tears ran down my face. Just as the others had, I started to scream. They electrocuted me again and again. Eventually, one of the men hovering over me took my dog tag, looked at it, and said, "Another fucking Jew! You know, they all have small cocks!" His partner sneered, "I know! Fucking Jews!" They both laughed and signaled for the man to shock me again. This happened over and over. At last, they stopped. "Okay," one snapped. "Go back to the other room." The ordeal was over.

Even though this was only a war game, the memory of it has stayed with me. My fellow GIs seemed to enjoy shouting anti-Jewish slurs. If someone could persuade me that lessons were learned, that the episode had made recruits better soldiers if captured, I might reconsider whether the incident was instructive. Even though it occurred in the middle of New

Jersey and the enemy was not real, the experience remains indelible.

That night remains the only time in my life when someone "attacked" me for being Jewish. I could not help thinking about the Holocaust, about all the real persecution that Jews had met with throughout history. This was not war. There was no danger. But I remember it well.

∞

Throughout my six months of service to Uncle Sam, I never stopped trading stocks. During this time, I came to realize what a passion I had for trading. Perhaps because I was in a more restricted environment, I found my greatest daily pleasure was following the market. By now, my portfolio had grown substantially. When I enlisted in the army, I entrusted the hands-on management of my money to my friend Eric Sheinberg, a fellow Wharton graduate who would go on to have an outstanding career at Goldman Sachs.

Occasionally, during my army days, Eric would drive to Fort Dix to visit with me and bring me margin and other brokerage papers to sign. I was not an exemplary recruit and therefore was confined more than most without a weekend pass. On one of these boring weekends, I decided it would be worth the risk to relive with Eric one of our dinners at school in Philadelphia. It would also be a kind of celebration because I was making money in the market while enduring the drudgery of army life. Unfortunately, army brass did not routinely hand out off-base dinner passes. Some army sergeants had regularly asked for my advice on how to invest their paychecks, but they would not reciprocate with special dining privileges. Having been taught by the army to be inventive, I persuaded Eric to smuggle me off the base under a blanket in the back seat of his car. The lobsters we ate at Bookbinders in Philadelphia that evening tasted that much more delicious for the effort.

In May, my army hitch finally ended. When I got my discharge, I immediately headed back to Wall Street, a place I had come to love even more in my absence. At first, I had a hard time finding a job. Then an agency landed me a staff-writer position at a publication called *Financial World*. I was happy to have the work.

# 5

# THE HOTTEST ANALYST
# ON WALL STREET

**M**Y JOB AT *FINANCIAL WORLD* HAD TWO COMPO-
nents. First, I wrote a weekly column called
"News and Views on Investing," which dispensed
general advice and information to our subscribers. I covered cyclical industries—those that produced
steel, agricultural equipment, automobiles, and similar staples.
I filled up one-third of the column, which amounted to a
handful of paragraphs, with as much factual material as I
could. I did not have access to specialized information, nor did
I break news. Mostly, I just scoured industry publications and
newspapers, and pulled together material from those sources.

Usually, I took a day to a day and a half to research and
write my part of "News and Views." For the rest of the week, I
had to do the second part of my job: answer subscribers' letters. *Financial World* offered its readers the right to write in and
ask its "experts" one question as often as once a week. The
subscriber would then receive a personal letter answering that
question. My duties included creating those reply letters, a
task I did without enthusiasm.

Some of the letters, especially those that were rather eso-
teric, were difficult to answer. Consider this one—made up, yet
representative:

Dear *Financial World:*

I own 36 bonds of the Lackawanna Railroad, which is the predecessor company to the Do Re Mi Railroad, and through merger has become an obligation of the Pennsylvania Railroad. I would like to know where these bonds presently trade, the history of their interest payments and arrears, and the taxable income for a holder since 1928.

And on and on and on, ad nauseam. As in this fictional case, many of these letters were extraordinarily specific with little actual analysis required. Usually, I had to plow through stacks and stacks of Moody's and Standard and Poor's reports until I found the answers to these questions.

I also got a number of letters like this one:

Dear *Financial World:*

I am a shareholder in General Motors. What do you think of that stock?

These were a pleasure to answer because they went to the heart of my interest: securities analysis. But, for every four GM-type letters I got, one Lackawanna-type letter would hit my desk. From the start, I had to force myself to answer some of them.

Soon, I dreaded dealing with the obscure questions so much that I began putting them in a special pile and devoted only one day a week to answering them. Then I began answering them even less frequently. Finally, it reached a point where I answered them only when I received an irate letter:

Dear *Financial World* [a complaining letter would begin]:

Cancel my subscription. You promised me you would send a letter in answer to my inquiries, and six weeks ago I sent you a letter about the Yuckayucka Electric Company to which you have not yet responded.

I would then diligently shoot back a reply:

Dear Subscriber:

Please accept our apologies. Your letter may have been lost in the mail, but here is our view on the Yuckayucka Electric Company.

One day, when I was home, sick with the flu, my boss saw that day's mail and discovered several complaining letters. To try to figure out what was going on, he rummaged through my desk until he found the drawer where I kept the unanswered letters. There they were, all stacked up neatly for him to see, ample evidence I had not been doing my job. When I returned to work, he called me into his office, looked me straight in the eye, and fired me. No questions asked. I tried to think of a way to explain why I had not been answering the letters, but I could not. Without a second thought, my boss told me to clean out my desk and leave, immediately.

Walking to the subway station, I thought, "What a disaster! Fired, and I'm only 22! How am I going to put *that* on my resume?" Later, on the subway, I worried that my career on Wall Street was over. "It was fun while it lasted," I decided, "but what a pathetic way to go. Fired—all because I could not force myself to answer a bunch of stupid letters."

Not a week passed, however, before my boss called and asked me to come back to work. It turned out that the person he hired to replace me had a drinking problem and did not return from lunch one day until four o'clock in the afternoon. I jumped at the chance to redeem myself, and told him I would be in the next morning. I felt an enormous sense of relief as I walked through the front door of *Financial World* that first day back. Life is fortuitous, at least sometimes.

When I was rehired by *Financial World,* I became a diligent worker. I felt that I had been given a second chance at having a career, and I was not going to blow it. I answered each and every Lackawanna-type letter the day I received it. When I got in the habit of doing this work, I found that reviewing the musty financial histories of companies could be peculiarly fascinating. They often provided graphic evidence of how mightily things change. Questions on obscure investments taught me about the large populace of unsophisticated, ill-informed investors who invariably find themselves owning securities that, over time, lose meaning and value to their owner. Many of these sad investment letters reflected the unspoken history of much of the financial world.

Despite my diligence, I still disliked the drudgery of having to answer those letters, so I started looking for another job. At *Financial World,* I had befriended a fellow stamp collector (stamps were a childhood hobby of mine) who introduced me to Joe Lasser, an analyst at Wertheim & Co. Joe and I began discussing investments. He took up my cause in seeking new employment. I guess I must have impressed him with my depth of knowledge.

Wertheim did not have any job openings at the time, so Joe introduced me to some of the senior people in the research department at Loeb Rhoades & Co. They arranged for an interview. I was thrilled that they would even see me. I met with several people on different occasions during the interview process: Richard Pollack, head of the consumer stock area and, later, all of research (he would eventually join me at Steinhardt Partners); and Sidney Knafel, who oversaw industrial stocks and ultimately was my direct boss (he eventually became an enormously successful private equity investor). Much to my delight, Loeb Rhoades offered me a job, which I immediately accepted. I was excited about leaving my dreary work at *Financial World;* I felt as if I had sprung an escape. Now I would have the chance to work at one of the premier brokerage firms on Wall Street.

I had been at *Financial World* for nine months and was fired once in the process. That was long enough.

&

I was 24 when I started working at Loeb Rhoades as a research analyst. At the time, Loeb Rhoades carried a great mystique. Like many Wall Street firms, it had evolved from a German–Jewish banking family. In the 1960s, many men employed there were Jewish immigrants—highly educated, articulate, urbane. These men, like Armand Erpf, Sam Steadman, and Mark Millard, created an aura. At the head of the firm stood the stately figure of John Loeb, a highly respected, albeit (for most junior employees) somewhat distant leader.

I liked the people at Loeb Rhoades, including the senior partners, but I particularly enjoyed my fellow research department colleagues, some of whom became close friends. I was in a young department. We all shared investment ideas and played the devil's advocate role for each other. Most of my fellow analysts had an enthusiastic entrepreneurial bent, and making money in their own accounts was as much a measure of their success as being appreciated by clients. We also had fun and real camaraderie. Often, we went out together after work.

Working at Loeb Rhoades also finally brought home the peculiar irony of my father's help. If I had gone to City College as I had originally intended—if my father had not shown up at the last minute and changed the course of my life by sending me to Wharton—Loeb Rhoades would never have hired me. Almost everyone at the firm had gone to an Ivy League college: Harvard, Yale, Penn, and so on. Wall Street, then and now, has always sought out people with elite educational backgrounds. Because of my degree, and thanks to my father's foresight, I could at least get my foot in the door. The rest was up to me. I have often wondered about the distinction between the pure academic elitism of the Ivy League schools and the relative academic excellence of the New York City schools of that period.

My job at Loeb Rhoades further changed my life: I was now being paid extremely well. Indeed, I was making considerably more money than anyone I knew—certainly anyone I knew from Bensonhurst.

I often worked well into the evening—sometimes until midnight—because doing this analytic work was a pure joy. I loved every day and enjoyed every challenge. I quickly established myself as a serious analyst who had an instinctive understanding of the inner workings of companies and even industries. Because of my experience at *Financial World,* I initially covered cyclical sectors. In analyzing individual companies, particularly in well-established homogeneous industries such as automobiles, I relied largely on a range of statistical input gathered from trade publications, car and truck sales reports, and an extraordinary plethora of other quantitative material. I regularly visited company management in Detroit. Moreover, my work required a thorough understanding of corporate balance sheets, historical and current, as well as patient reading of notes and references in corporate financials, annual reports, and SEC filings. Perhaps most important were the earnings projections this information produced. Relating these to broader economic change separated good analytic judgments from the pack. Analysts who took the time and had the energy needed to do this intricate analysis were generally viewed as the best researchers. A certain academic quality to the research at some firms detached that process from the immediacy of money making.

I took particular pride in estimating the quarterly per-share earnings of the companies for which I was responsible. One quarter, when I accurately predicted General Motors' earnings per share to the penny, I felt I had attained an ultimate achievement. Precise earnings predictions may be common events in this day and age. Back in the mid-1960s, they were rare feats.

The process of finding attractive investments through fundamental analysis, which included management visits and patient quantitative projections, was deeply satisfying. I loved writing reports that presented off-consensus positions, and visiting institutional clients and articulating views. I also took great pride in being proved right in both a company's fundamentals and its share price. However, there were times when I was right about one and wrong about the other.

∞

One day, John Loeb Jr. asked me to make a research visit to a conglomerate called Gulf and Western Industries. John had run into its chairman, Charlie Bluhdorn, at a cocktail party, and had arranged for an analyst to visit the company. Because Gulf and Western had a large auto parts division, NAPA, which I knew of, he selected me to meet with Bluhdorn.

Conglomerates were often freewheeling entities with dizzying growth rates. Many conglomerates participated in unrelated businesses through mergers and acquisitions. Loeb Rhoades had, until that point, an aversion to following conglomerates in their research coverage. The firm held the view that "internal" growth, as opposed to growth by acquisition, had far greater value, was much more predictable, and therefore was deemed more appropriate for its clients. Also, dealing with conglomerates required an understanding of "creative" accounting, which was often beyond the grasp of Wall Street analysts. Finally, many conglomerates attracted slick "wise guys" with dubious reputations. These managers often strained to create a connection between the old and the new businesses of their companies. They made efforts to articulate a philosophy that emphasized the managerial qualities that are applicable broadly, rather than the competitive edges that come from experience in only one industry. Some said that these diversified companies were stuck together by "chewing gum." Loeb Rhoades, conservative and old-line, felt these suspect companies were best left for other research firms to follow.

Bluhdorn, in particular, had a reputation for being one of the most ruthless conglomerate chieftains in America, but when I went to see him (I was then 25 years old), he seduced me with his cleverness. He was eccentric, feisty, and opinionated—a real tycoon and a brash gambler. He was known as "the mad Austrian" and, judging from his record, he was brilliant. My meeting with him was nothing less than exhilarating. He talked about the various diversifying strategies that Gulf and Western had employed to maximize the company's growth rate. He ranted and raved about the aggressive acquisitions he would make. He stomped his feet. He cursed. He was intense and animated. I left the meeting inspired, and immediately wrote a research report recommending the stock. In less than three months, the stock price tripled. My reputation as an analyst began to flourish.

Because of my success with Gulf and Western, Loeb Rhoades changed its view of researching conglomerates. I was soon asked to analyze other similar companies. Thus, I got to know the companies, and many of the CEOs, of the high-profile conglomerates of the day, such as Derald Ruttenberg of Studebaker Worthington, Nicholas Salgo of Bangor Punta, and Eli Black of AMK (which later became United Brands). I became friendly with George Scharffenberger, who had just left Litton (the birthplace of executive genius at the time), and started City Investing. Saul Steinberg, age 22, had created a company called Leasco, which leased computers. Leasco became a hot stock, took over an insurance company, Reliance, and eventually made an unsuccessful bid to buy, of all things, Chemical Bank! Jimmy Ling, Chairman of Ling-Temco-Vought, was in the process of acquiring companies at an unprecedented pace. The conglomerates were the darlings of Wall Street, and, for a period, I was their booster.

In fact, I believe I was the first to introduce the word "synergy" (the whole is worth more than the sum of the parts) in explaining the virtue of conglomerate investing. Of the six or so conglomerate stocks I recommended, all went up—sometimes dramatically—not long after I recommended them. It was as if I had a direct line to God. Several times, when I recommended a company, an imbalance of buy orders delayed the opening of the stock on the New York Stock Exchange the next day. For a time, it seemed I was the hottest analyst on Wall Street.

For the first time, I felt a certain power based on my own intellectual judgments. The financial world seemed responsive, and, because I was only in my mid-twenties, that power was certainly intoxicating. Still, even then, I realized that markets and people have their cycles, and my status as a hot analyst could not last forever.

∞

While I worked at Loeb Rhoades, I still lived with Harry Freund. Harry was in real estate, but I arranged for him to interview for a job in the research department at Loeb Rhoades. Ultimately, he was hired.

Living in the apartment with Harry, I no longer saw my mother on a daily basis, but I still saw her often and I was constantly trying to persuade her to move to Manhattan. I would take her to restaurants that I frequented for business dinners. I was proud to treat her to the best luxuries but, while she mostly enjoyed the dinners, she was appalled by their prices. She would say she preferred a good kosher hot dog.

During my years at Loeb Rhoades, I began to see more of my father too. Early on, he wanted me to invest for him. He would give me, say, $10,000, all in $100 bills. Naturally, I never asked where the money came from. I simply took the money and deposited it in order to begin investing for him. Occasionally, he would come up with more than $10,000. Once, he handed me a substantially larger amount, which I stuffed in my pockets. The subway ride back to my apartment was a little nerve racking. I had all of these envelopes in my pockets, stuffed with cash. It heightened my consciousness to be carrying stacks and stacks of $100 bills through the streets and subways of the city.

As always, there was a certain ambiguity in the relationship between my father and me. Were he and I partners in his investments? Were we going to split the profits? Was he simply lending me the money? He could and did ask me to return money, without notice, whenever he needed it. I, of course, paid full tax on all the gains, a factor that further complicated our arrangement. The truth was, neither of us had ever thought it through.

Investing my father's money allowed me to invest in the stock market without feeling undue pressure. Moreover, his "easy come, easy go" attitude about money led me to be almost oblivious of my own financial circumstances. Indeed, to this day, I do not know how (or why) to balance a checking account. For me, participation in the market simply offered the thrill of being right; the shorter the time span between investing and succeeding, the greater my fulfillment.

My gambling in the stock market was clearly a much better bet than the sort of gambling my father did. I enjoyed significantly better odds, and I always had a high degree of confidence that my investments would work. Somehow, it mattered to me that picking stocks, being a good analyst, and speculating had a purpose to it that truly distinguished it from my father's gambling. It was important to me to be doing something of value. As it turned out, I made my father a lot of money; yet, although I always gave him a handsome return on his investment, it was never quite satisfactory. Was this because of the ambiguity of our "deal," or because I felt that nothing I could do would ever be good enough for my father?

∞

After her divorce from my father, my mother dated, often on Friday and Saturday nights. She used to go regularly to Club 28, a place for singles over the age of 28. She would often come home with her girlfriends—other single women of her age. They would sit in the living room and go on and on about how terrible it was to go to places like Club 28 and meet men who had no interest at all in getting married. My mother believed that if a 40-year-old man was still single, there was something wrong with him. Nevertheless, in the universe of men my mother dated, a good number were over 40 and had never been married.

I remember one in particular—Sam, a little guy with a long nose, who was head over heels in love with my mother. Unlike many of her boyfriends, Sam wanted to marry her, and they had a real romance while I was at Loeb Rhoades. I was so much a star analyst that almost all of my recommendations were highly profitable. Sam apparently had some cash and wanted me to open an account for him. I was especially determined to make money for Sam, because of his relationship with my mother. I bought him one stock about which I was highly confident. It was fairly thin and volatile. Unfortunately, I misunderstood the amount of money he had available to invest and thought he had said to buy $24,000 worth of the stock when he only wanted $2,400. Not four days after I bought the stock, the price soared, as the prices of the stocks I picked often did. Sam made a 25 percent profit, but he could not pay for it, which embarrassed him to no end. I urged him to somehow find the funds to pay for the purchase because the profit was so large. As a broker, I could not help him because of legal restraints. Since he could not come up with the money, I was forced to transfer the shares to one of my other discretionary accounts, which meant he never benefited from the transaction. It was a sad, poignant episode, and it gave my mother some insight about the man she was dating.

⤬

Around this time, I became friendly with a young analyst at A.G. Becker, Howard Berkowitz. Independently, we both got involved with one stock, Allied Paper, and this brought us together. We began to focus on other stocks together and to share ideas. Again, this was a magical period in which almost everything I touched did well. Howard was similarly blessed. Eventually, he introduced me to a fraternity brother of his, Jerrold Fine, who managed the partners' capital at Dominick & Dominick, an old-line investment firm. We had all been at Wharton at about the same time, but I had not known either of them until recently. Each of us was in his mid-20s.

Howard came up with the idea that the three of us should start our own private investment fund—a hedge fund. None of us could predict where the enterprise would take us, but we were excited about the prospect of having a business of our own, a business in which compensation would be solely a function of our own achievement. It was a capitalist's dream. We knew it was our destiny.

First, we had to come up with a name, and this turned out to be difficult—perhaps more trying than picking the right stocks. Sitting around in Howard's apartment one night, we discussed whether we should use some sort of generic title or our own names. With some trepidation, we decided to use our own faintly ethnic monikers, but then the order of their placement was the subject of a long debate. You would think that three grown, seemingly mature men would not be concerned about the order of their names, but our egos stood out in front of us. Each of us made a case for where his name should be placed. Jerry finally opted out of the discussion by persuading us that Fine was the short name and therefore the logical pick to be in the middle. We accepted that judgment. Finally, Howard and I, after spending an inordinate amount of time discussing the issue of whose name would go first, flipped a coin. I won and our business was named Steinhardt, Fine, Berkowitz & Company. We thought it had a pretty good ring to it, and it certainly was a statement of our self-confidence.

We hired Paul Roth, Howard's brother-in-law, who had just started his own law firm–Baer and McGoldrick, which eventually became Schulte Roth & Zabel. We were their first hedge fund client, and they eventually became the biggest and best law firm in the hedge fund business. Paul was concerned that Steinhardt, Fine, Berkowitz & Company sounded more like a Jewish delicatessen than a money management firm. We used it anyway. Other than that one miscue, Paul's counsel over the next 30 years was nearly flawless.

# 6

# STEINHARDT, FINE, BERKOWITZ & COMPANY

O UR NEW FIRM WAS STARTED AT A TIME WHEN events forced my deepest attention elsewhere. The threat of the Jordanian-Egyptian-Syrian coalition that led to the Six-Day War exploded in the Middle East just as my partners and I were on the verge of launching Steinhardt, Fine, Berkowitz & Company. I wanted to think about the good prospects ahead, but this terrible event affected me deeply. My good fortune surely could not coexist with Israel's misfortune.

In retrospect, the Six-Day War turned out to be Israel's greatest military triumph. But in the weeks preceding the war, victory was far from certain. All of Israel's neighbors, led by Egypt's virulently nationalistic president, Gamal Abdel Nasser, were united in their determination to push the Jews into the sea. The world had not witnessed similar trauma surrounding Jews since the eve of the Holocaust. I needed to do something. I had been only a toddler during the Shoah. Now I was 27 years old.

The war broke out on June 5, 1967. The next night, I attended a mass rally outside the United Nations complex. Thousands of Jews, their faces etched with an ages-old panic for their people, filled the streets. One after another, politicians made speeches on the flat bed of a large truck. Jewish leaders begged the United States Government and the United Nations to come to the aid of Israel, which was fighting for its very existence. It was a moving rally, but a palpable sense of helplessness and terror tempered this moment of Jewish solidarity.

After several speeches, Shlomo Carlebach, a renowned, albeit controversial, rabbi and folk singer, got up on the truck bed. He had made a name for himself by helping troubled youth in the Haight-Ashbury district of San Francisco and, after his death years later, became the father of twentieth-century Jewish religious music. "The only thing worth saying now is a prayer for the Israeli soldiers who have died in the last 48 hours," Carlebach told the crowd. With this, he started to sing "El Malei Rachamim," the prayer for the dead. As his voice filled the streets around United Nations Plaza, the mob suddenly became silent. An unnerving calm filled the air. All that could be heard on Forty-seventh Street between First and Second Avenues was the deep, melodic sound of Carlebach's voice resonating between the buildings. Thousands of people stood in a collective hush. Finally, toward the end of the song, Carlebach could no longer maintain his composure. Giving in to the extreme emotion of the moment, he broke down weeping. While he cried, his sobs echoed between the buildings and created a tableau of pain and compassion that I will carry with me for the rest of my life.

Following the rally, I spoke with Carlebach, whom I had befriended years earlier. He told me he wanted to go to Israel to entertain and comfort the troops. I immediately agreed to pay for his trip. But this was not enough; I wanted to do more than finance another's contribution to my people. Just as when I was younger and had fantasies of saving Jews from Nazi or Arab hordes, I felt the need to do something physical to help fellow Jews. As the war began, with Arab threats and posturing, it looked like a fight for survival in which all Jews were needed to do their part perhaps for the very existence of Israel. I decided that nothing would be more meaningful than volunteering to fight to protect the Jewish state. Apparently, I was not alone. When I tried to reserve an airline ticket to Israel, I discovered that all the flights were booked. American Jews, as well as Israelis living here, clogged the airlines with last-minute efforts to get to Israel. Finally, I found a route via Olympia Airlines to Athens; once there, I would figure out how to get to Jerusalem. But before my departure to Athens, on the sixth day, the war ended.

∞

The news of the war delayed our opening Steinhardt, Fine, Berkowitz & Company until July 10, 1967, one month later than originally planned. We began with eight employees and an initial capitalization of $7.7 million, raised mostly from family and friends but also from a few intrepid individuals who were willing to speculate on three young upstarts. Almost all initial investors remained with us until the firm closed 28 years later. We opened our doors at 67 Beaver Street, not far from Wall Street. Steinhardt, Fine, Berkowitz & Company was in the hedge fund business.

We were not the first to create the hedge fund structure, although we certainly were early pioneers. A. W. Jones, a sociologist, started the first hedge fund in 1949. He combined the purchase of cheap stocks with the short selling of overpriced stocks and added leverage, and created a successful strategy that was intended to make money regardless of the overall direction of the market. The fund was considered "hedged" and the term "hedge fund" was launched.

By the mid-1960s, several offspring of the Jones model existed. When Howard, Jerry, and I thought about creating our money management firm, the hedge fund model appealed to us most. Unlike Jones's theoretical model, however, we never wanted to use hedging to eliminate all market risk. Rather, we counted on both our ability to pick stocks and to get the overall direction of the market right. Foremost, we wanted the flexibility to play both the long and short sides of the market.

I liked to say that, contrary to conventional wisdom, we created a conservative medium that used speculative techniques to ameliorate risk. Most traditional money managers at that time were nearly entirely invested on the long side and therefore had anywhere between 85 and 99 percent of their capital exposed to the stock market all the time. This works well when the market goes up, but when the market goes down, such investment vehicles invariably lose money. Our hedge fund sought to generate absolute positive returns for our investors, regardless of the direction of the stock market.

We also felt it was critical for each of us to invest virtually all of our personal wealth side by side with our clients. We were partners with them in each and every investment; their risks were our risks. Indeed, throughout my career, the great bulk of my personal net worth was always invested in my funds, and, to this day, I will not invest money with a manager who does not do the same.

Another notable characteristic of the Jones hedge fund model that attracted us was the lucrative fee structure. Traditional money management firms typically receive a fee of $1/2$ to 1 percent of invested capital. Hedge funds generally charge a management fee of 1 percent to cover overhead and expenses, plus a percentage of the profits—in our case and conventionally, 20 percent. Performance-based fees provided a money-earning incentive far in excess of asset-based fees. The bottom line: If our fund lost money, we would not get paid and our personal capital would suffer; if we earned substantial returns, we would be rewarded handsomely. We were young, confident, and willing to bet our future on making performance-based compensation our ticket to success.

From the start, Steinhardt, Fine, Berkowitz & Company did well. Of the many U.S. hedge funds that existed when we started in the late 1960s, we were one of the few that survived through the next decade. It was not the hedge fund structure that did most of the funds in; it was the market of the late 1960s and early 1970s.

∞

As we settled into the roles that would become more defined over the years, I focused more on trading, and Howard and Jerry concentrated more on securities analysis. Our business exploded. The firm posted a 31 percent gain in our first (three-month) fiscal year, and we realized a 99 percent gain in the second year (our first full year). For the Standard & Poor's 500, the comparative figures were a gain of 6.5 and 9.3 percent, respectively. By the end of fiscal 1969, Steinhardt, Fine, Berkowitz & Company had almost $30 million in capital, some of it amassed through profits and some of it through new investors. In two short years, still in our late twenties, Jerry, Howard, and I had become millionaires.

In a very real sense, we were the mavericks of the day. Around this time, a book called *New Breed on Wall Street* was published. The book described us as brash, gutsy, we-know-how-to-do-it-better-than-you-do guys who did not hesitate to challenge tradition. In the book, one photograph showed us playing bumper pool in our offices—an image meant to convey our bucking the establishment. An old-line, waspy, bow-tie crowd dominated the traditional Wall Street firms; we were renegades whose youth and cockiness were shaking the Street. Indeed, we expected our clients to invest with us *only* because we would give them better results. We either performed by achieving the highest of absolute standards, or we had no raison d'être.

I was quoted as saying: "We speak to the forty- and fifty- and sixty-year-olds and we understand this market better than

93

they do. We're more flexible, we understand values better."
Now that I find myself a geriatric 60-year-old, that observa-
tion seems rather arrogant and brash, but it proved pretty accurate at the time.

⸎

When we opened the doors of Steinhardt, Fine, Berkowitz &
Company in 1967, the U.S. economy was booming. These
were the Go-Go years, a period of euphoria on Wall Street.
The stock market was characterized by newly aggressive trading in and out of stocks by institutions, primarily, mutual
funds. As recently as the end of World War II, the mutual
fund industry had been a minor element in securities trading.
By the mid-1960s, it had become the transforming force on
Wall Street. Moreover, individuals began to increase their
share of equity ownership through mutual fund share purchases. There rose a cadre of "gunslingers": Gerry Tsai of Fidelity, Fred Alger of Security Equity Fund, Howard Stein
(following in the footsteps of Jack Dreyfus) of Dreyfus, Fred
Carr of The Enterprise Fund, and the notorious Fred Mates of
The Mates Fund. Long gone were the days when mutual fund
portfolio managers operated slowly, cautiously, prudently, as if
they were trustees. No longer married to their holdings, they
traded actively and turned over their portfolios rapidly. The
concept of unfettered growth—a new idea for equity investors—
became a substitute for value and for dividend yield.

In the Go-Go years, stocks were purchased in a fast, lively,
almost peremptory manner, sometimes with scant information.
All that was needed was a "story" that preferably could be told
in a nutshell and tagged with a name that captured it suc-
cinctly. At Steinhardt, Fine, Berkowitz & Company (or SFB, as
we came to be known), we were aggressive early buyers of
story stocks. We listened and quickly we got it.

We owned Maine Sugar, whose story sprang from growing sugar beets in Maine, thereby providing an alternative to potato growing in an economically weak area. Remarkably, that story was exciting at the time. National Student Marketing's story was the burgeoning youth market. Its stock eventually rose to over 100 times earnings. There were mariculture companies engaged in fish farming, and hydroponics companies growing plants in liquids. Computers, teleprompters, calculators, and digital watches were some of the biggest, hottest stories. Any enterprise that had the word *data* in it was seemingly worthy of purchase simply because it implied cutting-edge technology. Those players included Control Data, Mohawk Data, and Scientific Data. And then there were names that ended in *-onics* such as Liquidonics and Avionics. Four Seasons Nursing Centers and United Convalescent Homes would transform elderly care—a growing business, thanks to favorable demographics. Weight Watchers International could make you thin and rich at the same time. We owned them all.

Our biggest success came with King Resources, a company whose story was vast oil and gas discoveries as well as land holdings. We believed it, although in all fairness we were relying heavily on the promotional pitch of the company's chairman, John King, with whom we felt we had a real rapport. As King spoke more and more optimistically about prospects, the shares went higher. We made about five times our money in a few months. We eventually sold, only because it had gone up so much. In a few short years, this company, like so many other Go-Go sagas, would go bankrupt. I learned that a story, whatever its veracity, could be of value, particularly if it were new to the market and had an open-ended quality that provoked one's imagination. We listened to and were attracted to the most articulate, persuasive managers. Their stories, in retrospect, were often absurd; nevertheless, they easily caught our interest and the market's in this highly speculative moment. In some sense, we were the greater fools because we too got caught up in the euphoria of the period. However, in contrast to almost everyone else, we had an inner tension that came from viewing the portfolio anew with fresh minds every day. Thus, although we were believers, we sold.

∝∽

Around the time when we launched the hedge fund, the block trading business emerged on Wall Street. In block trading, an institution, such as a mutual or pension fund, calls a broker and attempts to buy or sell a large block of stock—say, 100,000 shares or more—in a single stroke without having to enter numerous smaller orders. Specialist firms traditionally played this liquidity-providing role on exchanges such as the New York Stock Exchange. However, as institutional investors became larger and more actively turned over their portfolios, there was a need for greater commitments of capital. Thus, some large brokerage firms got involved in facilitating these transactions and earned high commissions for doing so.

Some of the early stars in this newly created and highly visible arena were Jay Perry at Salomon Brothers, Bob Mnuchin at Goldman Sachs, and Willy Weinstein at Oppenheimer. It was a fast-paced, nerves-of-steel, highly competitive game. In matching up buyers and sellers and using their own capital to round out the difference, these block traders sometimes deployed huge amounts of money and took meaningful risks. Because I had an active portfolio and was prepared to trade (largely on the basis of "market input"), I talked regularly to each of them throughout the trading day. We developed a real trading camaraderie. In one sense, I was a natural ally, but, because I was at the center of this trading information, I gained a competitive advantage. We had direct lines to the trading desks at each firm. I wanted to get the block traders' first call when they had indications of stocks to buy or sell in size. Knowledge was power in the trading world. Like other hedge funds, we were often accused of "running ahead"—trading on the knowledge of buyers and sellers that the block traders provided.

In the early days of block trading, I sometimes felt I was taking candy from a baby. In 1969, a trader needed to sell 700,000 shares of Penn Central, a large railroad in the Northeast at that time. The stock was already in Chapter 11. I was shown a block of stock in the third market. I then checked the New York Stock Exchange Market, where it was trading at $7\frac{7}{8}$. The seller must not have bothered to sufficiently explore the market makers' book on the Big Board because I bought 700,000 shares at 7. In fact, the seller seemed relieved to have sold that amount of stock at less than a dollar under the last trade. Meanwhile, I turned around and sold the 700,000 shares at $7\frac{3}{4}$ to a buyer at another firm. I could have sold three times that amount as the buyer was significantly larger. I made more than a half million dollars on a trade that took all of eight minutes. On top of everything else, the transaction was relatively risk-free. Those opportunities are gone now. They reflected a transitional period, a window of opportunity, in the market when there were few players as nimble and as wired as we. That window is long closed.

Sometimes making money was due, not to intelligence or courage, but to simply "being there." I tried to view my role in the firm on many levels. One was the commitment to take advantage of all opportunities, all the time, a focus that made every day an opportunistic trolling seeking with each phone call some way to ring the cash register. It was in no sense inconsistent to have a cerebral conversation with a first-rate economist on some long-range economic phenomenon and in the next conversation get a pitch from a trader who had a large block of stock. Relative to our size we generated vast commissions for the brokerage community. This enabled us to get many advantages as a priority client. In retrospect, I am not as sure of its value. However, I am sure that the world perception that we were open to virtually any idea was, on balance, a big advantage.

Around this time, I first met Alan Greenspan. Then a consultant to Donaldson, Lufkin, Jenrette, he visited our offices every quarter with our DLJ salesman. I recall being disappointed that I had learned little from listening to him, and that what he said was mostly an extrapolation of the obvious. What can I say about him in retrospect? That he was a conventional, middle-of-the-road economist at that point? That he would grow a great deal in the future? There were certainly no clear signs back then that he would one day rule world financial markets.

∞

When I think back over my three decades-plus on Wall Street, I remember most vividly the experiences that were the most painful. Perhaps it is my nature, or perhaps I have always been my own harshest judge, but in those early days, I certainly made my share of mistakes. To this day, I will often ask a money manager what his or her biggest mistake has been so far. I have found that the best traders seem to remember their failures better than their successes, as do I. One of my earliest and perhaps most horrific experiences occurred when I shorted Occidental Petroleum (OXY).

The company was run by Armand Hammer, a too-clever man of myriad international conspiracies, and a superb promoter whose statements were often far too optimistic. I knew the company well, had traded in it successfully several times, and had decided, for reasons such as my bias against CEOs like Hammer, that the stock had become overvalued. I started shorting it in the mid-20s and continued, painfully, averaging up into the 30s. But the worst was yet to come. Before I could grasp what was happening, the stock spiked. Rumors abounded of a major discovery in Libya with speculation that the reserves discovered would rival Saudi Arabia. In a matter of a few days, the stock more than doubled. I was beside myself. The position represented only a small portion of our portfolio; nonetheless, it was excruciating to find myself so dead wrong about a stock that I thought I knew so well. The loss seemed enormous, and I was deeply upset. Whenever you lose on the short side, it is that much more frightening because the loss is theoretically without limit.

Each tick of the action in OXY preoccupied my every thought and dwarfed all other positions in the portfolio at the time. Moreover, I could not make a clear judgment as to whether this supposed discovery was any more substantial than others the company had been rumored to have made in the past—discoveries that never panned out. Alas, promoters sometimes get lucky too. I was a young money manager who had just lost a vast amount of money, and with that came a comparable loss of conviction. Estimates of a multibillion-barrel find abounded. I was in no position to dispute this.

I was sitting at my desk at 67 Beaver Street after the market closed one day. Feeling morose and utterly defeated, I stared out the window. I was paralyzed. Howard came in, and, while he too was pretty down in spirits, he did not feel quite as bad as I did. This was my position and my responsibility. He tried to be consoling, but I would not respond.

As the sun set, I continued staring out the window. Soon my friend from Goldman Sachs, Eric Sheinberg, with whom I was having dinner that night, came in, saw my mood, and, in a singularly annoying way, tried to be upbeat. He said silly things, like, "Relax, Mike, you still have your fingers and your toes."

When he said that particular line, I looked at him and said, "Well, how about testing yours?"

I glanced sneakily at Howard. Together, we opened the window and then grabbed Eric and told him of our intention to hang him by his thumbs out the window. He could not get away from us, try as he might, as we carried him toward the window.

Eric panicked. The loss in OXY had made me seem unpredictable, irrational, even violent; anything was possible. He started to scream. As we got closer to the window, in an outburst of energy, he finally broke away. We all began to laugh, and the dour mood was broken, at least for the moment.

# 7

## JUDY

I MET MY WIFE, JUDY, IN 1967, THE SAME YEAR we opened Steinhardt, Fine, Berkowitz & Company. Peculiar circumstances surrounded our meeting. Phil David Fine (no relation to my partner, Jerry), a Boston lawyer who had been affiliated with the Kennedys and was then the head of the Small Business Administration, had been close to Judy's family for years and knew that Judy had recently left Boston for New York. He was the brother of a friend and had given me her phone number some months earlier, but, because I was a shy bachelor who avoided blind dates, I had not gotten around to calling.

Previously, Phil had called to tell me that he was coming to New York because he had arranged for the girlfriend of one of his West Coast clients to perform at The Latin Quarter, a trendy New York nightclub. Phil was a close friend of the Walters family, especially Barbara Walters's father Lew, whom he had approached to get his client's girlfriend the gig. Appearing at The Latin Quarter was a big deal, so the favor Phil had arranged for his client, a man who ran a hot franchise company called International House of Pancakes (IHOP), was special. Phil invited me to the singer's premier performance, and in Phil's party that evening was Judy.

This was not the first time I had met her. After starting Steinhardt, Fine, Berkowitz & Company, I was still living on East Seventy-ninth Street and drove a car pool down to Wall Street. Every day, I picked up three (sometimes, four) friends. My apartment was near Lexington Avenue. Going east, I picked up one friend at the corner of Third Avenue, another at Second Avenue, and another at York Avenue. Then I'd drive us all downtown.

In the car pool was my current girlfriend, with whom I had worked at Loeb Rhoades. There was also a girl who lived on York at Seventy-ninth Street and had two roommates. At some point, one of her roommates fell in love, got married, and left the apartment, creating an opening. The girl who controlled the apartment's lease, Barbara Eisenstein, of Wilkes-Barre, Pennsylvania, had a distant friendship with Judith Abrams, who grew up in Scranton, Pennsylvania. They had renewed their friendship and traveled together to Israel after the Six-Day War. At the time, Judy was working in the Boston Redevelopment Authority, an urban renewal agency, but had decided she wanted to move to New York. When Barbara's roommate left, that created an opportunity for Judy—the same Judy Phil knew—to come to New York.

An aside: The roommate who had left, making room for Judy, was Denise Eisenberg. She went to Spain to be with the man she subsequently married, Marc Rich, who later became an investor and then a good friend of mine. Marc Rich, of course, was one of the world's most famous fugitives, but all of that would come later. In the mid-to-late 1960s, Marc had a different life, one that obviously intrigued Denise Eisenberg. Judy took Denise's room in Barbara's apartment. The phone number Phil Fine had given me, which I had not called, was Judy's.

The oldest of three daughters, Judy had come from an upper-middle-class family in Scranton. Her father was a rack jobber who supplied supermarkets with drugstore-type items. Ultimately, he sold his business to A&P, but even when Judy was young, he made a good living. Following a tradition among the women in her family, Judy attended the University of Michigan and then earned a master's degree from Tufts University. That's how she ended up in Boston. When she came to New York, she got a job in Mayor John Lindsay's administration—again, in urban renewal.

Judy took the subway to City Hall during the period when I picked up her roommate Barbara every morning as a member of my car pool. My girlfriend would sit in the front seat of my navy-blue Plymouth Fury convertible, and Barbara would sit in the back, along with Andre Elkon, also an analyst with Loeb Rhoades. At that time, I was the hottest of stock pickers and was about to leave Loeb Rhoades to start Steinhardt, Fine, Berkowitz & Company. As I drove the car pool, my passengers pressed me for stock tips. "What are you buying, Mike? What do you like?" Some mornings, our whole conversation as we headed downtown would be about my favorite stocks.

Not long after Judy moved in with Barbara, she went skiing and sprained her ankle. Barbara asked if I had room for Judy in my car for a few days. It was a long walk from York Avenue to the subway, so it would be easier for Judy to simply hobble outside her apartment, where we would pick her up. I agreed and into the car one morning came Judy, who proceeded to sit in the back seat of my car and don a huge pair of black sunglasses. I glanced in my rearview mirror to catch a glimpse of her and immediately thought she looked enchanting, faintly resembling Audrey Hepburn. She was tall, had dark hair, dark eyes, and the brightest smile. Judy did not say one word to me or to anyone else the entire time she rode in my car pool. Each morning (I took her down to City Hall for a number of mornings in a row), she sat in the back seat of my Fury convertible in regal silence, looking beautiful. I felt no need to hear her speak; peeking at her through the rearview mirror was enough.

Years later, Judy would insist she made money from being in my car pool those few days. She heard me talking about Maine Sugar Industries and Colorado Milling Company, and, after a day or so, she called her father to tell him she had met this "stock market genius" who recommended these two stocks. Apparently, her father bought the stocks and made so much money when their prices skyrocketed, as I said they would, that he rewarded her with her first fur coat.

I did not say anything to Judy. When she got out of the car, though—with some difficulty, because of the sprained ankle—I could not help but notice how attractive her legs were. This went on until her ankle got better and she no longer needed a ride to City Hall. Much later, Judy told me she had asked Barbara why she had never fixed the two of us up, and Barbara replied that she did not think I was Judy's type. Judy apparently went out with tall, social, preppie types—not quite my description. What Judy had not told Barbara was that, because of the way her parents had talked about different professions as she was growing up, Judy had a leaning toward Wall Street men. Some parents implore their daughters to marry a doctor or a lawyer, or so the cliché goes, but Judy's parents seemed to prefer a nice Jewish financier. Judy, however, did not have even a slight interest in finance herself.

At The Latin Quarter, I had my first chance to focus on Judy alone. When I did, I became enthralled. As we sat in the club, we exchanged strained, idle chitchat until we were comfortable enough with each other to dance. I will never forget holding her in my arms on the dance floor. She was radiant, angelic. She was also graciously diplomatic, never mentioning what a terrible dancer I was. And I *was,* and am, a terrible dancer. My own crummy dancing was the last topic on my mind, however. By the end of the evening, I could think of nothing but Judy. She swept me away. She was and is a vision of beauty and charm, of brightness and spirit.

Not long after the night at The Latin Quarter, I got up my courage to call Judy and ask her out. Happily, she accepted. On the evening after Rosh Hashanah, I picked her up at a friend's house in Westchester County. We drove to the home of my friend, Rabbi Shlomo Carlebach, whose family lived in an apartment above his synagogue on West Seventy-ninth Street, between West End Avenue and Riverside Drive. Shlomo's parents were there, and Shlomo and his mother, a dignified and imperious woman, engaged in hilarious dialogue. She intimidated him, but whatever her criticisms, and there were many, he always responded with a smile. He was innately respectful but had a mischievous gleam in his eyes. After the evening's festivities, Judy and I left Shlomo's and walked along the Hudson River. On Rosh Hashanah, Jews are supposed to walk beside a body of water and figuratively throw their sins into it. Judy and I performed no rituals—neither one of us was knowledgeable enough—but we enjoyed ourselves on this Rosh Hashanah. By the end of the night, I was thoroughly infatuated.

∞

If I did not fall in love with Judy during that night at The Latin Quarter, then I certainly did on our first date. It was almost love at first sight. Immediately, I broke up with the girl I was dating and started seeing only Judy. We became serious right away. One of our favorite ways to spend an evening included strolling through Carl Schurz Park, situated in the 80s along the East River in Manhattan. Gracie Mansion, the Mayor's residence, is located nearby. On one evening, we walked through the park and it started to rain lightly. I asked Judy if she minded walking in the rain and she swore she did not. She seemed so natural. It was one of those glorious moments that happen early in a relationship—two people walking through a misty rain, not feeling a drop, falling more deeply in love. In all the years I have known Judy, that was the only time she walked unprotected in the rain.

Some nights, I gave Judy quizzes on geography or politics. I would ask her to name the capitals of places like Cyprus, South Africa, Bulgaria, and Ethiopia. Most often, the answers lay just outside of her reach, as I had intended. I guess I needed to establish superior knowledge. Judy never lacked for conviction and was perfectly comfortable with what she knew and what she did not know. I think she preferred my distant knowledge in areas like geography and politics because she knew what really mattered. We began to play tennis together. More often than not, I won. I provoked Judy by saying that her mother taught her that sometimes it was better to lose to certain men. She rigorously denied this.

Judy was a traditional liberal Democrat and, while I did not consider myself a Republican (though I did vote for Goldwater in 1964), I was proud to say I was a conservative—a rarity among Jewish New Yorkers. I read the *National Review* with enthusiasm; I admired William Buckley. I took pleasure in teasing liberals, which included most of my friends. In some sense, my conservatism was a response to much of what I did not like about New York. I did not believe the answer to the city's problems was increased government spending. Like contemporary conservatives, I thought the answer rested in tax cuts, incentives for private enterprise, and reductions in the public sector. I would rant about the welfare system and Johnson's Great Society programs. Judy and I had many arguments about politics, but only in retrospect did I learn how unimportant the topic was to her.

We dated throughout the fall. By the end of the year, I worked up the nerve to ask her to marry me. She accepted and we were married on April 28, 1968—altogether, a whirlwind romance. The wedding took place at Glen Oak Country Club, near Judy's home in Scranton, and Shlomo Carlebach was one of the two rabbis who married us. Shlomo, a bearded, Ortho-dox hippie, bothered Judy's mother, whose lifestyle reflected a more assimilated and Americanized version of Judaism.

My future mother-in-law hired Lester Lanin's Orchestra, one of the preferred bands of the Upper East Side WASPy so-cial elite, to play at our wedding. She picked him because he epitomized high society, which she greatly appreciated. At the rehearsal dinner, I remember Judy's mother herding around what she perceived as my inelegant, "schoolboy" groomsmen from Brooklyn. Of course, they were my oldest and dearest friends, and I was happy to have them with me. In contrast, Judy's aunts were all intensely aware of the correct etiquette as dictated by Emily Post.

My father, free from the social constraints of Judy's mother, had his own idea of what a wedding should be. At one point during the reception, he walked over to the orchestra leader and asked him to play some traditional Jewish wedding music, which had been noticeably absent. My father had a way with words. "Hey," he said in his deep, gruff voice, "play some Jewish music."

The bandleader looked at my father. "I'm sorry, Mr. Steinhardt," he said, "but we were told not to play Jewish music." He *had* been told this too, in no uncertain terms, by Judy's mother.

So my father, without subtlety, reached into his pocket, re-trieved the wad of cash he always carried, and dug out a $100 bill. "Now play some Jewish music," he said, handing the bill to the bandleader.

The stunned bandleader would not take the money. Nor would he play Jewish music. Befuddled, he glanced around until Judy's mother came over to find out what the problem was. When he told her, Judy's mother turned to my father and told him flatly, "I'm in charge of this wedding, Mr. Steinhardt, and there will be no Jewish music. Now that's that."

My father gave up, clearly defeated. Beating out my father was no small feat, but Judy's mother had done it. I can think of few other people who did.

This was, astonishingly, the second time Judy's mother had won a confrontation with my father. Some weeks before the wedding, my father announced to Judy's mother that he wanted to buy the champagne for the reception. He did this because he only drank one brand of champagne, Dom Perignon. If he could pay for the champagne, he would be guaranteed to have the brand he wanted. Also, he felt compelled to contribute financially to his son's wedding, whatever the tradition. The message seemed to be: my father viewed Judy's mother as a country bumpkin. Judy's mother took my father's gesture as an insult; not only was it traditional for the bride's family to pay for the wedding, but the Abrams family was at the apex of Scranton society, both socially and financially. Thus, my father's proposal was totally and rigorously rejected. My father had met his match.

After we were married, we moved into my bachelor apartment on Seventy-fifth Street between Madison and Fifth Avenues. Harry had already married, ending our rooming together. Within two months, Judy was pregnant. Thus, we needed more space, so we started looking for a larger apartment to buy. Within months, we bought a penthouse duplex with a stunning view of Central Park and the Upper West Side beyond. The building, on the corner of Fifth Avenue and Ninety-seventh Street, remains our home today.

We were still in the process of remodeling the apartment when our first child, David, was born, on March 3, 1969. Being married had brought joy to my life, and having a child only made that joy more profound and purposeful. In my life, I would be fortunate enough to have much success. However, nothing I accomplished in the world of finance would ever match the feeling I experienced when I cradled my son David in my arms for the first time. I must admit I unabashedly rooted that our first baby would be a boy and my joy was compounded when I saw the deep, familial cleft in his chin.

∞

Happily, Judy and my mother loved each other from the first moment. They would often gang up on me to complain about my bad habits; being late and eating too much were the prime targets. Throughout my life, I have been plagued by almost always being overweight. I come by it naturally. For most of their lives, my mother, father, and most of their siblings were too heavy. When I feel frustrated and even guilty about my lack of weight discipline, I comfort myself with the finding that 90 percent of people with two overweight parents are destined to be overweight themselves. Nevertheless, in an era in which you apparently can never be too skinny, I continue to fight a lifelong battle to permanently lose weight. I have not succeeded, despite my mother's and Judy's best efforts.

From the moment I earned my first dollar, I sought to enhance my mother's life. After living in Bensonhurst for years, she finally moved to Manhattan in the late 1960s. Her new home was The Vermeer, a rental apartment at Seventh Avenue and Fourteenth Street. She lived there only a short time before I bought her a cooperative apartment in The Brevoort, an attractive building on Fifth Avenue between Eighth and Ninth Streets. The building was going co-op at the time, so I bought the apartment from the sponsor. His sales agent was a woman who seemed to be as tough as nails. She offered a no-compromise, take-it-or-leave-it attitude, which, in my case, totally succeeded. Her name was Leona Brown. She later married Harry Helmsley.

To me, buying the apartment did not begin to repay my mother for all that she had done. I had felt that many of the hardships in her life, and the sacrifices she made, reflected her

111

singular devotion to me. I still feel that nothing I will do could ever repay her love and devotion. My mother never wanted much in the way of material things, and she became uncomfortable if thrust into a fancy environment. When I took her out to a fine restaurant and she thought the prices were too high (she almost always did), it nearly ruined the meal for her. She insisted on shopping at S. Klein on the Square, a now-long-gone department store in Union Square. Klein's distinguishing attraction was bargain prices. Later, when I was earning amounts of money beyond her grasp and was willing to supply her every want, her habits, carefully nurtured from years of thrift, would not change. Yet she was excited and proud to bring her many friends to her new home. I took great pleasure when I sensed that she appreciated the apartment. I longed for the opportunity to make her happy, to balance the scales for all she had done for me.

In 1969, not long after Judy and I married, my mother went on a cruise and met a wonderful, kind man named Mark Deskin. He was one of the original mechanics in the first Ford Motor Company plant in New Jersey. Mark and my mother had a sweet, autumn romance, and, within a year, on Christmas Day in 1970, they married. My mother's marriage made me almost as happy as she was. She would now have her own life with a husband to take care of and a husband who would take care of her. I knew how central I had been to her life, and I was happy to see her share her life with someone else. Nothing was more important to me than her happiness, but I could do little to affect her happiness other than to simply be her son. When she married, that changed; she focused on Mark. My duty now would mostly be to help them financially. She had not been married for almost three decades; she and my father had divorced in 1941. Through all these years, she had been socially active at times, but she was basically alone. She now had a husband in her life again, one far more responsible than my father.

Mark was a simple man, but so handy that he could fix anything. His ability to repair things like cars, appliances, and toys was remarkable. I am mechanically inept so, later on, my children would turn to Mark for help when they had banged up their bikes, go-carts, and other playthings. Mark could fix all of them. The kids adored him. After Mark and my mother married, they first lived in my mother's apartment in The Brevoort but soon moved to Florida, where they bought a house in Margate. My mother's new happiness was a blessing.

∞

Fairly early in our marriage, I realized that Judy had an innate commercial streak. Her eyes would light up when she discussed the relative attractiveness of merchandise offered in clothing stores. She could also turn this fascination into some commonsense advice, telling me I should buy this or that retail stock based on what she saw in their stores—not unlike what Peter Lynch was doing at Fidelity.

I particularly remember her urging me to buy stock in The Gap at one point, when she was constantly buying clothes for the kids there. She told me it was going to be an extraordinary success, and she was absolutely right. To my regret, I bought no shares.

In the late 1970s, Judy also convinced me that Americans were about to become more sophisticated in their food shopping and would appreciate a far broader range of delicacies. We were going to become a nation of gourmets. Judy had decided that she wanted to set up a hydroponic farm. Together, we settled on the idea of growing *fraise du bois,* the strawberry one finds as a rare and expensive delicacy in France and Italy. We concluded that if she could supply New York City, on a year-round basis, with fresh *fraise du bois,* it would be highly profitable. So, we traveled through Israel and France, learning about the business of strawberry growing and marketing, particularly of the Alpine strawberry.

Upon our return, we financed an experiment, at the University of Connecticut in Storrs, to grow *fraise du bois* hydroponically. Unfortunately, the experiment never reached fruition. Undeterred, we bought a hydroponic greenhouse that used the waste heat from one of New York's utilities in Queens. Abandoning the *fraise du bois* idea, we grew lettuce, tomatoes, melons, and other produce. Finally, with the help of some brilliantly conceived marketing from Milton Glaser, Judy developed a special approach to selling basil and other herbs. Calling her products Herbs Alive, she conceived of selling them still living, with the roots attached. Herbs quickly became our main crop.

With great enthusiasm, Judy would go to local supermarket chains and restaurants selling her fresh basil. She had considerable success, and the business grew. Unfortunately, profits did not. Moreover, the project consumed a great deal of her time. Ultimately, we decided to continue being only food consumers.

The cliché about a woman's role and a man's role certainly applied to our family. Judy handled the innumerable details of running a household. She focused on the kids' nutrition, their clothes, the schools and camps they went to. I happily went along with her decisions. Her efficiency contrasted glaringly with mine. In some sense, the intensity that I devoted to my business consumed almost all the energy I had. I was left with almost no discipline for our family life.

Whatever my intellectual pretensions, I recognized that Judy's judgment of people far surpassed mine. For so much of my business life, I was the bestower of vast commissions and other financial benefits that attracted many social relationships but rarely yielded close friendships. I was easily finagled by charm; Judy was far more discerning of a person's character. Too many times, I made bad errors about people and their underlying motives before I was set straight by Judy. Her social skills and outgoing personality have kept us a popular couple, perhaps too popular, all these years.

One of the more traumatic periods for parents in New York (and elsewhere) is the time of college applications and acceptance for their progeny. In our world, the competitive intensity and the ego involvement can be appalling. We were not immune; we hoped that each of our children would be accepted at the best possible school that was appropriate for his or her talents and desires. The anxiety leading to special tutors, worry about SATs, college application essays, and more, is familiar to many parents and is perhaps compounded by the pressured environment of the Upper East Side of Manhattan. Happily, our kids did well. David was accepted at the University of Pennsylvania and Daniel at Duke. Both schools had been my sons' first choices.

Sara has always been an exceptional student. Perhaps because she has two older brothers, she has demonstrated a remarkable maturity from early childhood. When it came time for her to apply to college, Sara made an early application to Yale. Judy was plainly excited by the prospect of a "Yalie" daughter and, when Sara was accepted, Judy was exuberant. She told everyone we knew, and, almost immediately, traveled to New Haven where she acquired virtually every appropriate article of clothing with "Yale" or "Y" embossed on it. Her purchases must have set a near-record at the Yale campus store.

As I had learned in the markets, life too often takes unpredictable turns. Before long, Sara seemed unhappy with her choice. She said that while Yale was okay, the broader environs were deeply unappealing, particularly when compared with New York, which offered more cultural and intellectual opportunities. Judy was devastated; she was also apprehensive about restarting the application process this late in the spring. Sara then appealed to me, perhaps because I could never refuse anything she asked. A late application was made to Columbia, and she was immediately accepted. Sara was ecstatic.

We had not heard the full story yet, however. Nearly two years before, I had interviewed David Berman, then at Harvard Business School, to hire at Steinhardt. I liked him and offered him a position. As part of the interviewing process, I invited him to Shabbat dinner at our home, where he met all of my family. David refused the job, preferring an offer in Los Angeles, where he had lived after emigrating from South Africa. David kept in touch during his year of work in L.A. One day, he called to say that he would be in New York and would like to meet. Judy, Sara, and I joined him for brunch and, before long, he joined the firm. Unbeknownst to Judy and me, our daughter had fallen in love. She preferred Columbia and New York not for cultural or intellectual reasons, but simply because she wanted to be near David. Her parents remained blissfully ignorant until December of her freshman year, when David asked for our permission to marry Sara. Nothing in our married life compared with the raw astonishment on Judy's face when she heard that her 18-year-old daughter wanted to marry. David and Sara were married 18 months later. They have two beautiful boys, Jacob and Joshua, and their "Nana" has all but forgotten about Yale.

Day to day, week to week, and year to year, Judy has been the rock in my adult life and the glue that has held our family together. She ran our family, making sure that we all functioned. I must admit, I complicated this job considerably by being unable to leave my moods, based on performance fluctuations, at the office. When I came home during a bad period—ironically, a bad period was determined only by my unrealistic demands on myself—my suffering would be there for all to see. Judy played a critical role in helping me prevent my moods from affecting our family life at home too much.

This was rarely easy, especially because I often did not recognize my own mood swings.

Judy has an innate balance; she was truly centered in contrast to my volatility. Fortunately for our family, Judy was and is hardly ever prey to mood swings, even those that might have been precipitated by her husband. She rarely lost her temper with me, a fact for which I remain profoundly grateful, and she remained steady under most pressures. Ultimately, Judy was a better and more consistent mother than I was a father.

She still plans all of our trips. Her planning often gets down to the microscopic level. She handles with ease the complex orchestrations needed when our kids head in all different directions. I am of little help in that regard. I must confess that I have never once packed my own suitcase, a fact she does remind me of at times. I deserve the reminding.

More than a few times, on seeing us, people have confused Judy with my daughter, a fact I have not always taken so well. She has truly retained the beauty and charm she had when I first met her. I am profoundly blessed that she has been with me to share life's vagaries, for the most part happily, for more than 30 years.

# 8

# VARIANT
# PERCEPTION

I N 1970, WE BEGAN TO EXPAND AT STEINHARDT, Fine, Berkowitz & Company. We started an offshore fund, SP International S.A., for foreign investors; our initial capitalization was $2 million. Over time, it would grow to more than $3 billion. But back then, our assets under management, both onshore and offshore, totaled about $35 million.

Our office on Beaver Street was too small to have a trading room, and we did not need one when so much of our work remained research-oriented. We did, however, manage to find room for a bumper pool table, which was used quite regularly. We often played pool after the markets closed, or sometimes well into the evening, and discussed the day's battles while we released tension. When analysts from the brokerage houses came peddling their research, we often challenged them to a game and developed greater insights and intimacies as we played. Remarkably, people seemed to play pool in ways that parallelled how they traded and invested. Jerry was quite classic, direct, and accurate. Howard sported great technique and was perhaps the most reliable player. I, who had never held a cue before, always looked lame. However, I learned to adapt, particularly by emphasizing defensive strategies, blocking holes, and frustrating my opponents.

Another pastime to let off steam was liar's poker, a game involving betting and bluffing with the serial numbers on dollar bills. Unlike the Wall Street titans of the late 1980s, who reportedly played for millions, it was a bad day if one of us lost more than $10 or $20. In this game, as in trading, judgment, courage, and perhaps a thespian's mien, were critical.

Around this time, we hired Frank Cilluffo, known to us as "Tony," who had worked at Arthur Lipper and Company, the major broker to Investors' Overseas Services (IOS), the large group of mutual funds that invested in other mutual funds. "The Fund of Funds" had been founded by a notorious promoter, Bernie Cornfeld, who asked potential clients the infamous question: "Do you sincerely want to be rich?" Cornfeld was highly successful throughout the 1960s, until IOS turned out to be somewhat of a scam and made those who had invested with him sincerely poor.

Tony smoked no less than three packs of cigarettes a day. He was an extraordinarily intense person who held trading views with almost religious conviction. He was as thin as I was chunky, and he had a slew of idiosyncrasies. For example, his choice for lunch would remain precisely the same, as long as we were making money. During a good stretch, he might eat a unique culinary combo, such as a cream cheese and olive sandwich, for weeks at a time. When we had our next losing day, he would change his order and begin to eat the same peanut butter and banana on toast—or whatever selection was working—for a stretch. On a really good day, he might order two servings of the same item. Regardless of our success in markets, he consumed mostly cigarettes and coffee.

More than anyone I have met, Tony had the courage to make market calls *in extremis,* regularly predicting dramatic change. In a stock selling at 80, a market favorite, he would say, with a spiritually inspired conviction, that in a year it would trade at 10. He seemed to thrive on radical visions and often did not concern himself too much with articulating rationales. When playing liar's poker, he reveled in long shots. His bet would shock his companions by its bravado and would lead to endless challenges. He won at liar's poker often enough to at least *seem* respectable. Tony played a vital role in the firm. We also hired analysts Oscar Schafer and David Rocker. They too contributed importantly to the firm, but in a far more conventional way.

❧

In the 1970 market break, when the Go-Go years finally ended, we established our reputation as a maverick hedge fund. This was when the "garbage stocks" and leveraged conglomerates of the late 1960s were annihilated. Many of the former "story" stocks that we had owned—the stocks we made a lot of money from, being long—we now turned around and shorted.

Short selling is a bet on a stock's decline. It involves borrowing shares from a broker in order to make a sale of the securities that one doesn't own. It takes a peculiar mental juxtaposition to become familiar, and at times friendly, with corporate management while supporting their endeavors, and then reverse and short the stock. It feels sometimes like rooting against the home team, like when my father rooted for the Reds at the Polo Grounds. Emotional issues—and questions of loyalty or credibility—are not always easy to reckon with in this situation. Ultimately, management contacts, who may have viewed you as an ally, can become hostile when they know you are short their company's stock and are anticipating deterioration. Needless to say, the rapport, the information flow, quickly dries up when you are viewed as an adversary.

For the first time since the inception of the firm, we went net short, meaning that the value of the securities we sold short was greater than the value of the securities we were long—something almost unheard of in the money management world back then. We shorted stocks like National Cash Register, Memorex, Intel, and University Computing—often at prices well over $100—and we covered some at prices under $10 per share. While we continued to believe that many of these companies were making real technological breakthroughs that were here to stay, we were simply dealing with questions of valuation. Far too many stocks were trading at prices—that is, multiples of earnings—that were too optimistic. And some, such as Four Seasons Nursing Homes, were simply outright frauds.

During this period, many of our hedge fund brethren, who had viewed short selling mostly as cosmetic, or had suffered the exquisite pain of being short overpriced flyers and not enduring it, performed poorly. Or maybe the euphoria of the times simply engulfed them. We stayed short and traded actively from the short side, and this tactic more than offset our own long-side losses.

An article by Carol Loomis, in *Fortune,* listed the top 30 hedge funds and discussed the difficult times most were having in the market. (Some of the largest funds had declined by 70 percent.) We were the only hedge fund on that list that would still be in business 10 years later. Moreover, investors soon grew uncomfortable with this new investment vehicle, the hedge fund, and massive withdrawals from many funds followed. However, our success in this period seemed minor compared with the money we made during the demise of the Nifty Fifty era.

The Nifty Fifty were the glamour stocks of the early 1970s. They were the favorites of the "star" portfolio managers at such reputable old-line institutions as Morgan Guaranty, Bankers Trust, U.S. Trust, and the like. Investors believed that because these companies had extraordinary growth histories and prospects, they were "one-decision" stocks—you could buy them and never sell them. There was no price or multiple too high to pay for companies such as Avon, Xerox, Polaroid, and McDonald's.

This was a period in the stock market, and in economics generally, when people believed in their ability to make accurate long-term predictions. They were reflecting the distinct optimism of the times. It was not unusual to read research reports with earnings-per-share estimates stretching out 20 and 30 years, particularly for one-decision companies. This further fostered the comfort in paying record-high multiples. If there was a fad during that period, as there often is in investing, it was to believe that growth per se, largely unconstrained by valuation, achieved investment results greater than other traditional criteria.

We rarely played the Nifty Fifty stocks from the long side. We had an aversion to paying high multiples even when we were sufficiently persuaded of the growth prospects. It seemed to us that unless one could realistically seek the expansion of a multiple as well as earnings growth in a long investment, it wasn't worth doing. Further, we never had the "religion" of the institutional-fund stars who made these one-decision stocks. These managers truly believed that investors could own the top growth stocks forever. We knew no investment was sacred and this led to a perpetual skepticism, perhaps even an indiscriminate skepticism toward companies about which others waxed euphoric. Indeed I have never thought that any stock or style of investing is of the one-decision type, especially not when valuations become extraordinary, as they did during this period. If the Nifty Fifty fad was ever going to end, it was inevitably going to end badly. We wanted to make sure that we would profit, not suffer, from it.

I remember when the Dow first closed above 1000 in the fall of 1972. The Nifty Fifty were the leaders. We were net long about 50 percent; we were positive on the market but were deploying our capital somewhat conservatively. By the time the averages peaked a few months later, we had sold out most of our longs and again gone net short.

125

One of the rules of shorting stocks is that you have to sell on an "uptick." The rule was imposed to help achieve stability in periods of sharp market declines. This necessitates establishing a short position while there are still plenty of buyers in the market. Therefore, to establish a short, you sometimes have to be a little bit early. Being early means you often have pain before you make money. For one fiscal year (1972), we underperformed.

This period created considerable tension within the firm. We were short the "best" companies in America—a frightening prospect. Eastman Kodak, General Electric, Johnson & Johnson, Coca-Cola, McDonald's—we were short them all. These companies were growing, were competitively advantaged, and had outstanding management and high visibility—perhaps everything one would want in a long investment. We had just one overriding basis for being short: price. I must acknowledge that classic short selling would not favor price as the determining factor. Textbook short selling would necessitate finding securities with deteriorating fundamentals, weak competitive positions, vulnerable dividends, and leveraged balance sheets (in contrast to companies on the typical list of the institutional favorites). Who were we to predict when this overvaluation phenomenon would end? How high was high? In some sense, what we were doing was counter to most investment logic.

We would buy a value stock—a secondary retailer such as Vornado—at eight times earnings and watch its price decline so that it was trading at six times earnings. Simultaneously, we would short a Nifty Fifty retailer like Sears Roebuck at 30 times earnings and see the multiple expand to 40 times earnings. Thus, we would lose on both trades. Yet, with fits and starts, with many sleepless nights and internal disagreements, we largely stayed the course. In this respect, Tony, with his unswerving vision that was not subject to the rational arguments of the moment, proved particularly helpful. Being

126

short the Nifty Fifty was the truly contrarian view, and when views are truly contrarian, they are inevitably uncomfortable. Courage and the ability to withstand pain are required.

By the time the Nifty Fifty finally started to break in 1973, it was often too late to get an "uptick." The bear market that started then was not a panic, as in 1929, but it certainly was tedious and relentless. Day after day, month after month, the market kept going down. Brokers would call us because they were trading a block of stock. They knew we were short that stock and wanted us to buy back or "cover" on their trade. We passed and stayed short, often waiting patiently to cover much later when the prices were even lower and the position traders were selling out. During this period, even some brokers to whom we were paying hefty commissions started to resent us for making money when everyone else was losing. People questioned whether short selling was un-American and innately manipulative. Management whined about how short sellers were beating up their stocks.

In 1973, the Dow was flat and we were up about 15 percent. By fiscal 1974, when the market was down 38 percent, we were up 34 percent. Most of the former "hot" institutional portfolio managers at the major banks lost about 50 percent when the Nifty Fifty tanked, but even they fared better than many of the "star" mutual fund managers, some of whom lost a startling 80 to 90 percent. People began referring to us as greedy and arrogant. Nothing gives a better feeling to a money manager than making money for his or her investors when almost everyone else is losing. That was, for me, the height of professional satisfaction.

In an absolute sense, there are two reasons why profit in a down period, from short selling, can never match the magnitude of a comparable success on the long side.

For one thing, all that one can make on a short is 100 percent of one's investment. Perhaps more to the point, the mentality of most short sellers allows only for more modest potential gains. Moreover, profits from short transactions, however long they are held, are treated for tax purposes as short-term transactions.

Still, nothing feels better than the psychic joy of having protected one's capital while disasters abound.

By the time the Dow hit bottom (577, in December 1974), it had lost almost 50 percent of its value from its high of over 1000 in January 1973. Yet, even the Dow averages did not reflect the carnage that was taking place within the overall market. By then, bearishness was rampant and people were afraid to own stocks. However, because we had been so successful during this debacle, we had great confidence in our view that the market was sufficiently pessimistic to create a bottom. Just as outright euphoria is often a sign of a market top, fear is, for sure, a sign of a market bottom. Time and time again, in every market cycle I have witnessed, the extremes of emotion always appear, even among experienced investors. When the world wants to buy only Treasury bills, you can almost close your eyes and get long stocks.

In late 1974, flush with both our relative and our absolute success during the previous two years, we picked the market bottom nearly perfectly. Again, this was augmented by the genius of Tony, whose judgments remained unerringly accurate. During this period, he truly had a direct line to God (if indeed there was one).

In the course of one month, we switched our net exposure from minus 55 percent to plus 35 percent—a huge reversal from short to long. We would have gotten much more aggressively long had we been able to find fundamentally attractive choices fast enough. Somewhat randomly, we bought a broad basket of single-digit stocks (stocks that were trading under $10 a share) with institutional names that had been decimated in this bear-market period. Market timing dominated, and we did not have enough time to do serious research or to easily make the necessary mental switch. We just knew we wanted to put money to work in the market quickly. Thus, we were a little indiscriminate regarding the names we bought, but many of our purchases were trading at 75 to 80 percent of book value with price-earnings multiples of around seven times earnings. We owned stocks like Howard Johnson, Zapata, Bath Industries, Suburban Propane, and Tropicana. We bought them right and, as usual, we sold them early. That year, we were up about 66 percent.

<hr />

During this period, I began to consciously articulate the virtue of using variant perception as an analytic tool. I defined variant perception as holding a well-founded view that was meaningfully different from market consensus. I often said that the only analytic tool that mattered was an intellectually advantaged disparate view. This included knowing more and perceiving the situation better than others did. It was also critical to have a keen understanding of what the market expectations truly were. Thus, the process by which a disparate perception, when correct, became consensus would almost inevitably lead to meaningful profit. Understanding market expectation was at least as important as, and often different from, fundamental knowledge. As a firm, we soon found that we excelled at this. We took exactly that approach during the early 1970s, when most of our success resulted from our implementation of perceptions that were meaningfully at variance with consensus wisdom. We shorted near the top, in the face of great bullishness, and we got long at the bottom, in the face of keen pessimism.

Having a variant perception can be seen benignly as simply being contrarian. The quintessential difference, that which separates disciplined, intensive analysis from "bottom fishing," is the degree of conviction one can develop in one's views.

Reaching a level of understanding that allows one to feel competitively informed well ahead of changes in "street" views, even anticipating minor stock price changes, may justify at times making unpopular investments. They will, however, if proved right, result in a return both from perception change as well as valuation adjustment. Nirvana.

∞

Naturally, we did not always get *everything* right, even in this period of incomparable success. And, because investing invariably requires making judgments with incomplete or often inaccurate data, there were times when we came precariously close to disaster.

One day, in March 1973, Jay Perry at Salomon Brothers called to offer us a very large block (400,000 shares) of Equity Funding, a stock we thought we knew quite well. We had been interested in part because of our favorable view of the life insurance industry. Tony looked at the chart and said, "Unless there's something really wrong, this stock is a great buy at this level."

Its price, $18, was approximately the 10-year low. In addition, Equity Funding management had stated publicly that it knew of no business reason for the recent decline in the price of its stock. We purchased 100,000 shares when the block traded at $17.50.

No sooner did the block trade than another broker offered us another block of stock. Then some convertible bonds also came for sale. We began to sense something was wrong. Dan Dorfman, who wrote the column "Heard on the Street" for the *Wall Street Journal,* called and asked me if I had participated in the first block of stock that traded. I said yes; we had in fact bought a good chunk of the stock. After a long pause, he mysteriously said, "You know, Mike, not all the pretty girls are as pretty as they look."

Shortly thereafter, trading in the stock was halted. The next day, the scandal broke. It turned out that Ray Dirks, a well-respected Wall Street insurance analyst, had received a tip from a disgruntled former employee that the company was creating bogus insurance policies by the thousands and then selling those policies, for cash, to other major life insurers. This information was unquestionably insider and material. Instead of going to the Securities and Exchange Commission to report the irregularities, Ray called his closest institutional clients, who, naturally, started dumping the stock. What was surprising, many people at the company knew about the fraud, yet they managed to deceive not only Wall Street but the auditors as well.

When trading resumed two weeks later, the stock opened at $6. Equity Funding had been a scam. The founder of the company, Stanley Goldblum, was convicted of fraud and eventually went to jail, but the enduring precedent for Wall Street involved the analyst, Dirks. He thought he had acted prudently but, to the SEC, he had profited by passing on inside information. He was eventually cleared by the Supreme Court, but the Street reeled from the scandal for years.

This was by no means the first time we had invested in a highly promoted company that ultimately was fraudulent, but it was the only example of our actually buying shares from sellers who, we soon recognized, had a significant information advantage. Inside information is a subject that can be philosophically approached in many ways, and its legal complications are constantly evolving. We kicked ourselves for months for having fallen for the scam.

There were other times when my instincts nearly got us in trouble. In late 1975, after being unerringly accurate on both the stock market and individual stocks for three years, we became bearish again, far too soon. Indeed, we were more net short than ever, and our performance suffered as the market continued strong.

Again, we were fighting the world and inadvertently were short the world's "best" companies. Each day was a battle. We traded actively from the long side to try to offset the net short exposure, but it wasn't enough. One of the few long positions we held (for well over a year) was in Studebaker-Worthington, a company I had known well from my earlier conglomerate days at Loeb Rhoades.

Like many other conglomerates, to "maximize shareholder value" and raise cash, Studebaker had issued shares in a number of its publicly held subsidiaries. Our small holdings in several of these subsidiaries included Clark-Gravely and Turbodyne. We also held a substantial stake in STP, a maker of motor-oil additives. One day, in mid-January of 1976, anxious, yet determined to increase our net short exposure without adding any more stocks to the short side of the portfolio, I saw a chance to unload our STP at a rich price, so I sold our conspicuously large block of stock to one buyer.

That evening, I attended a cocktail party given in honor of Senator Ted Kennedy. At this point, I had moved sufficiently to the left politically to be mildly enthusiastic about the Democratic Party. I looked around the room and saw Derald Ruttenberg, the CEO of Studebaker. I walked over and greeted him, and the moment he saw me he asked whether I was the one who had sold the large block of STP that day. I said, a bit embarrassed, "Yes, I was."

He looked me straight in the eye as if he was about to say something, then stopped himself, took a breath, and said, "Hmmm." I waited for another comment, but he just turned and walked away.

Later that night, I kept thinking about his "Hmmm." Was it a bad or a good response? Was there any meaning to be deduced? My instincts told me something more was going on.

The next morning, as soon as the market opened, I gave orders to buy shares in each of Studebaker's six public subsidiaries, including STP. Because most of the companies' shares didn't trade very well, I was unable to purchase many shares. Then, around noon, an announcement suddenly appeared on the tape. A trading halt had been issued in each of the companies I had placed orders in and had been buying throughout the morning.

I immediately realized that indeed I had made a bad sale the day before, and the few shares I had bought that morning were of no consequence. Later that day, Studebaker announced its intention to repurchase, at a premium price, 100 percent of the outstanding shares it did not already own, in all five of its subsidiaries. I felt like a fool, but markets often make you feel that way. Things, however, got even worse.

Within days, I received a subpoena from the Securities and Exchange Commission regarding my orders and purchases of all the subsidiary shares. The SEC was obviously concerned that I had been privy to inside information. A month or so later, I appeared before the commission to answer its questions. The SEC asked whether I would place orders simply based on a "Hmmm."

I answered, "Absolutely; instincts are often all one has."

They found it hard to accept that I would buy shares based on such an ephemeral conversation, but, in the end, they must have believed me because I never heard from them again.

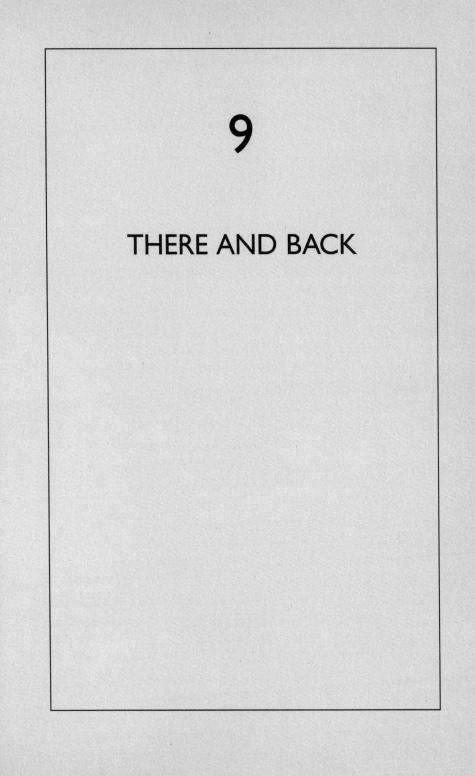

# 9

# THERE AND BACK

URING THE 1970S, THERE WERE BLESSED EVENTS in our family. On June 6, 1971, Judy gave birth to our second son, Daniel, a beautiful boy who throughout his childhood gave me great joy. He became the athlete that I never was and certainly had the most infectious sense of humor in our family. Then, on February 10, 1975, Sara was born. She was a freckle-faced blonde who would grow up to have a love of animals that more than matched my own. Despite my accomplishments in the markets, nothing I did could match the three creations I care about most: David, Daniel, and Sara.

In 1976, Jerrold Fine decided to start his own firm, Charter Oak Partners, which he based in Westport, Connecticut. When he left, Howard Berkowitz and I renamed the company Steinhardt, Berkowitz, & Company. Around this time, we also moved our office to midtown, 90 Park Avenue. In theory, I could now walk to work.

As of 1978, I had been in business for a little over a decade. In those years, I had made more money than I had ever dreamed possible. My net worth was more than $7 million, which may not seem like much money today, but it certainly felt like enough for me back then. (When did the term "millionaire" lose its meaning?) At some point in 1978, I began to realize that I did not have to work anymore. I could take my $7 million, invest it wisely, and live off the proceeds. In hindsight, that would not have been a decision I would have been happy with today, but it seemed attractive back then.

Introspection intensifies during times of success because one has the luxury of self-reflection. In 1978, I felt that, in my overall investment career, I had accomplished most of what I had set out to do. For me, the learning curve had flattened.

Perhaps because of the liberal socially egalitarian environment in which I grew up, I viewed varying professions on a vertical scale of values. Being a doctor seemed of far greater worth than being an accountant. To me, heroes were people like Dr. Albert Schweitzer, Albert Einstein, and David Ben-Gurion, none of whom was rich but each of whom had enriched the world. I was making rich people, including myself, richer—certainly not a sin, but not a qualification for sainthood either. I once received a picture of a beautiful yacht from one of my investors. The picture was captioned: "I bought this with the money I made from my investment with you." Here was the proverbial "customer's yacht," but somehow I was not gratified.

Having devoted almost all of my conscious energy, from my teenage years onward, to the stock market, I questioned whether I could ever do anything else with the same degree of competence. There were very few role models to suggest that I could. Indeed, almost everyone I knew who was successful on Wall Street continued to work beyond his or her need for additional wealth. When asked why they stayed, I often heard hollow expressions like "Because I love the game," or "It's the only thing I know," or "It's a way to keep score." Most successful businessmen continue working in their later years, and many become passive philanthropists. I was not quite sure what I was seeking, but I knew I wanted to do something different.

Adding to my dissatisfaction was the fact that I was not in the best physical shape. I chain-smoked cigarettes, especially during the trading day, when I constantly felt considerable tension. I was overweight, topping the scales at 220 pounds. There was hardly an approach, a diet, pill, book, shrink, nutritionist, or spa, in the United States and abroad, that I had not tried. I had been hypnotized and I had experimented with acupuncture. Once, I even had a balloon put in my stomach. I convinced myself that I worked too hard to allow for exercise. Almost every day, I ate lunch at the trading desk, certainly not a location conducive to a moment's respite. Why waste an hour going to a gym or out to lunch, and possibly lose the rhythm of the trading day? Because I approached each day as an opportunity to make money, the nonstop trading intensity, with its inevitable successes and failures, often left me physically drained. None of this was conducive to my health.

I devoted extraordinary energy to trying to understand my weight problem. For years, on particularly bad days, I would leave the office with an almost uncontrollable desire for nuts. I would tell my driver to take me to the corner of Eighty-sixth Street and Third Avenue, where I would visit the Treat Boutique. I would buy a quarter pound each of macadamias, raw cashews, shelled pistachios, and pecans. Each came in its own small separate bag. Immediately, I would consume some of each of these treats and, within minutes, I would feel a palpable decline in my level of anxiety. I would feel remarkably rebalanced. It was an opiate. Was I chemically addicted to fats? I think so. Whatever the case, the nuts worked, and I needed to ingest them, regardless of their effect on my waistline.

My daily schedule had an inherent repetitive quality: get up, go to the office, and do the same activities over and over. Every investment is unique and contributes to a continuing high level of intellectual excitement in the stock market, but a similarity of process, no matter what the investment, is unavoidable. I had not become "burned out"; I had simply grown tired of the process. I needed something else in my life.

So, at age 38, I made a radical decision. Having been in business for 11 years, I decided to leave Wall Street. At the end of our fiscal year on September 30, 1979, I was going to walk out the door of Steinhardt, Berkowitz, & Company and not come back.

Filled with anxiety and, at the same time, flush with excitement about what I was about to do, I went to my partner, Howard Berkowitz, and told him of my decision. We had a long philosophical discussion about both his and my future. Several days later, Howard met with me to suggest that it would be in everybody's best interest to view my decision as a one-year sabbatical rather than a retirement. This allowed the business to continue uninterrupted, gave me the opportunity to explore a range of alternatives, and left open the option of coming back. Further, it committed me to offering Howard a future comparable opportunity. His plan made sense and I accepted it.

I left the bulk of my personal money in place because I was confident that the firm would do well even without me. My best investment opportunity lay right where my money currently was. Steinhardt, Berkowitz, & Company had, by far, outperformed any conceivable alternative. On the last day of September, when I left my office, I did not think I would ever return. Indeed, almost immediately and without much difficulty, my full attention turned elsewhere. The stock market quickly became a thing of the past.

❦

As I anticipated my new life, I explored wide-ranging alternatives. One was politics. Around this time, the Jimmy Carter White House offered me the chance to head a commission studying the feasibility of creating interstate banking in the

United States. Most banks had charters to operate only within one state. The result was a multitude of relatively small banks that could not succeed internationally. In essence, the commission's charge was to validate and create interstate banking. American banks could then better compete with those of our major global trading partners where no more than a few huge institutions dominated. I visited Washington and met with Orin Kramer (a White House aide who ultimately became a money manager) and tried to generate my own enthusiasm for the project. I could not.

Other opportunities briefly surfaced. For a period of time several years earlier, I had been a member of New York City's Municipal Advisory Commission, at the invitation of Harrison Goldin, the City Comptroller. After I left Steinhardt, Berkowitz, the Comptroller asked me if I would be willing to manage the investments of the various city pension funds, which at the time exceeded $10 billion. The city's finances were still precarious; earlier, the city had barely avoided bankruptcy. I was excited by the thought that my investment skills might benefit the city I had lived in all my life and loved dearly. Indeed, if I could increase the return by even 1 percent, it could mean, in theory, at least an additional $100 million to improve teachers' salaries or expand budgeting in other areas where the city was consistently short of funds. After researching the many constraints in managing funds for which the prime beneficiaries are municipal employees, I realized that I did not want to be in the business of managing anyone's money anymore.

When I turned these jobs down, I solidified my conviction that I no longer wanted to be involved in markets. For a while, I went out of my way to cut myself off from any part of the financial community. I stopped reading the *Wall Street Journal*. I no longer followed the markets. For a period, I even ended most contact with my friends at Steinhardt, Berkowitz, &

Company. Surprisingly, despite my love of the market and my devotion to the firm, I did not miss being in the game—and that realization shocked me.

∝

Now, with plenty of free time, I did things I had been thinking about doing for years. First, I spent more time in Bedford, a town in Westchester County. We had rented houses there for almost a decade and finally decided it was time to buy. Judy and I had grown to love the area. Peaceful and bucolic, it is still close enough to New York City to allow commuting.

When we bought the house in 1978, the property included 16 acres. We were fortunate enough to make contiguous purchases so that eventually we owned 52 acres. One of the particular attractions of the property was water: a stream ran behind the house, and the entire piece of land backed up to a tributary that flows into the Croton Lake Reservoir. I was, and am, enamored of water, being near it, walking around the edge of it and sometimes simply looking at it.

Around this time, we also joined the Century Country Club, in Purchase, New York. German–Jewish families had founded Century, perhaps the most prestigious Jewish country club in America. The classic Stephen Birmingham book, *Our Crowd,* focused on some of these historic families. We joined with the hope that our children would make new friendships and enjoy a host of new activities at the club. We had some misgivings about bringing them up in the city, which offered a less child-friendly environment than Bedford.

A magazine called *Westchester* published an article about my "retirement." It included a picture of me, taken near the root cellar on our property. The article, titled "So, What's Missing?" explained that I had quit the financial world, which was remunerative but perhaps not sufficiently fulfilling.

I was determined to spend more time with my family. I especially enjoyed activities that I never had time for before. When we were in New York, I could not wait to get up in the morning and walk my older son, David, to his school, St. Bernard's, located on Ninety-eighth Street, one block away from our apartment. Some days, when I knew David would be playing sports with his class in Central Park, I would sneak across the street and hide behind the trees so David could not see me watching him. I knew he would be embarrassed if his classmates saw his father creeping around the park. I savored the simple pleasure of watching my son enjoying himself in gym class. I felt unrestrained love for him but, in characteristic fashion, harbored a certain competitive spirit as I watched him in his athletic activities. I rooted for him to achieve the athletic superiority I never had. From early on my emotional ties with my firstborn have been intense. There is no finer son than he and we have always been close, yet, I hoped to express my feelings better than I did. Still, whenever I could, I went back secretly to the trees.

On some days, I had absolutely nothing on my schedule. I felt a new freedom, in contrast to my prior life. New York is a cornucopia of possibilities and the options are limitless: going to museums, afternoon movies, lectures, and more. Before long, however, I sensed that the rest of the world was busily engaged in worthy tasks. I was uninvolved, and a peculiar sense of guilt began to settle in.

I began to schedule activities that opened up a wide range of new interests. I took yoga in a class of six students; I was the only male. I took piano lessons and learned how to play well enough to pick my way through "March of the Wee Folk." Many mornings, I took tennis lessons from 8:00 to 10:00 with a Croatian tennis pro who became a good friend. Often, we drove out to Queens and played at Tennisport. I loved tennis, but I frequently said that nobody had put as much time, energy, and money into becoming a better tennis player and had achieved less than I. I was, and, sadly remain singularly mediocre. I also started jogging but quickly decided it would never be my métier and quit after a few weeks.

Once a week, I was a Torah student with Shlomo Carlebach's twin brother, Eli, a rabbi whom I remember mostly for his sense of humor. This was one of my many efforts to become more comfortable with my religion. I found many of the sessions intellectually provocative, but many of the stories were like folklore, such as the meaning of the sneeze in relation to human mortality. Biblical distinctions between the races shocked me. Overall, faith continued to elude me.

Early in 1979, Judy and I had taken several trips to Israel. It struck me then that perhaps the best way for me to contribute to the Jewish future was to invest directly in Israel. Specifically, I came to believe that if there was to be a stronger bond between Israeli Jews and the Diaspora—the Jews living outside of Israel—the Diaspora needed to invest in businesses in Israel, but that relationship had to be based on sound business and profit potentials. Israel would then come to rely on investors, not handouts. With this in mind, I went into partnership with an Israeli businessman, Lehu Veisser. We constructed small industrial parks in the development towns, including Kiryat Gat, Natirot, Schderot, and Ofakim, that had been built near the southern borders of Israel primarily for strategic purposes.

These relatively small development towns were mostly peopled by new immigrants from North Africa. They were what Zionism was all about. The places we built attracted manufacturing facilities—bottling plants, plastics manufacturers, and so on. Many were owned by Jews from foreign countries. This seemed like a constructive contribution toward building the future of Israel. When I went to these towns, I was excited. I felt the motivation for this financial commitment was as noble as any Jewish commitment at that time could be.

If I had stayed longer with these investments, I would have no doubt made money. But Lehu and I had different business styles, so I eventually sold out. While I did not make money, I felt, in the deepest sense, that it was nonetheless a worthwhile endeavor.

During this period I met Shimon Topor, who eventually became a partner of mine. He became my guide to all subsequent investments made in Israel, some of which have been substantial. The results have been consistently successful in part because he has helped me turn down many that I was emotionally drawn to.

∝∞∽

All of my activities—and, on some days, the absence of any commitments—kept me content through the end of 1978 into 1979. But as 1979 moved along, I slowly came to realize that I did not want to leave the financial world permanently after all. Gradually, I began to miss the stock market. Most of my friends and colleagues were surprised that I had been able to stay away from Wall Street month after month, without even thinking about or trading the markets. They had expected that I would be drawn back sooner. I was not. For most of the year, I had no contact with the financial world and enjoyed many fresh opportunities. Yet, during my year off, I had found nothing as enticing or as intellectually provocative as the market. I had to conclude that the stock market, and perhaps *only* the stock market, uniquely suited me and my particular set of talents.

I returned to work on October 1, 1979, the first day of the new fiscal year. In my year off, I had come to understand that leisure time in itself was not something I could be totally at ease with. Indeed, I am not sure that I enjoy lying on a beach or being in a boat at all. Unless my life's pursuits had goals and purpose, they became marginal. I also came to realize that while being a money manager was perhaps not near the top of my self-defined "vertical scale of values," it could provide the means to achieve other goals. We all rationalize. I was rested and rejuvenated. I was a more complete person culturally, religiously, and emotionally. I had a new determination in life.

In my absence, the firm had done well. I shared in the profits for the year away, mostly because I had left my money with the firm. I did, of course, receive a reduced percentage of the general partners' compensation. In the weeks leading up to my return, when it became clear I was coming back, key changes took place within the firm's personnel. Some people wanted to stay; others wanted to leave. The most important change: My partner from the beginning, Howard Berkowitz, decided he wanted to start his own hedge fund. When I returned on October 1, 1979, Howard left to start HPB Associates, and my firm was renamed Steinhardt Partners.

When I resumed trading, I found that investing in the market was a welcome intellectual change from what I had been doing. On the first day back, having not picked up a trading line for a year, I felt insecure about my ability to get back into the dynamics of the financial world. But after two or three phone calls from the usual brokerage suspects, I felt as though I had never left. I realized that, during my year off, I had found nothing that fit my personality as comfortably as playing the market. Whether I was responding to the gambling aspect of the experience, or the performance-oriented goals, or some combination of elements, I was excited to be trading again. Once I was back in the game, I realized how much I had missed the adrenaline rush. It was exciting. It was, I could now conclude, what I wanted to be doing with my life.

Overall, the results of what I came to call "my sabbatical year" were ephemeral. But I did feel that when I returned to the business, I had to have a new rationale for doing so. My new goal was to build a hedge fund that was importantly different and larger than any that had previously existed. Having had terrific performance as a smaller fund, I would try to do the same with much more substantial sums of capital. One of the historic truisms of the hedge-fund world is its overriding diseconomy of scale in the management of money. The ability to achieve superior performance often begins to decline as one manages more money beyond the intellectual breadth of a manager.

Thus, there was an advantage in having one's money managed by a firm that did not primarily seek growth in assets and was not paid a percentage of the *assets* but only a percentage of the *profits*. Throughout our first years in business, we had virtually no marketing efforts. Growth was simply a compounding of our own internal performance. As we looked back on our superior performance throughout the 1970s, which averaged over 30 percent annually, we felt that we had a big structural advantage because we were the right size. Indeed, we felt a certain virtue in having turned away vast amounts of new capital.

∞

Upon my return, one of my first efforts was to raise new money from investors. I felt comfortable that our firm could now successfully handle a larger capital base with no loss of performance; also, I needed a new and exciting challenge to justify my coming back. Recent changes in the rules governing private investment partnerships (like our hedge fund) now permitted fiduciaries to expand their investment universe. This was the cutting edge in the world of private investment partnerships, and we worked closely with our attorney, Paul Roth, to get it done.

I asked John Levin, one of the best strategic thinkers among my general partners, to spearhead this fund-raising endeavor. Our goal was to raise $10 million, which, at the time, was a sizable addition to the $60 million we had under management. At first, it seemed like a preposterous idea. I remember John's query: "Institutionally, who on earth is going to invest with us?" Most institutions, such as endowments and foundations, had not heard of hedge funds, and when they learned that we used leverage and short selling, they were more than skeptical. Nonetheless, I was convinced there was an opportunity.

Our initial effort led to some internal battles among partners in the firm. Some felt that the fund-raising endeavor was a huge distraction because we now had to spend considerable time marketing ourselves. Until this point, our only marketing effort consisted of a few trips to Canada and Europe when we were launching our foreign fund, SP International, in 1970. Mostly, our investors had come to us via word of mouth. Indeed, we were variously constrained in taking in new investors by restrictive legal and partnership issues.

I was perplexed and amused by the reaction of the fiduciaries that John pitched. Was it not more conservative to hedge your market risk with a vehicle that could make money in up *and* in down markets? Had we not proved ourselves in the 1973 to 1974 debacle, when the traditional old-line institutional managers got clobbered? Was not the lack of correlation of returns with the stock market a selling point?

The first positive response came from Larry Tisch, who had been one of the original investors in Steinhardt Partners. Larry has always been an independent thinker, and he has an innate appreciation for value. Perhaps more important, he was also a friend. He agreed to commit some pension-fund money from two companies that he controlled: Loews Corporation

Claire and baby
Michael, Bensonhurst,
1941.

Claire and Sol
Steinhardt, Coney
Island, 1940.

Michael at his Bar
Mitzvah, 1953.

Sol Steinhardt at
Western Wall, 1975.

At 67 Beaver Street, original offices of Steinhardt, Fine & Berkowitz, 1968.

With Jerry Fine and Howard Berkowitz (© 1968 Cornell Capa, Magnum Photos, Inc.).

Twentieth anniversary of Steinhardt Partners, LP, Temple of Dendur, Metropolitan Museum of Art, 1987.

Dedication of Steinhardt School of Education at New York University, Larry Tisch (trustee), Jay Oliva (President, NYU), Judy Steinhardt, Michael, Anne Marcus (Dean, Steinhardt School of Education), Martin Lipton (Chairman, Board of Trustees), April 2001.

Michael and Judy, opening of the Steinhardt Conservatory, Brooklyn Botanical Garden, 1988.

In Bedford with David, Judy, Sara, and Daniel, 1991.

Michael in his office, 1995 (James Estrin/NYT Pictures).

With Jack Nash, Odyssey Partners, 1991.

At the Falkland Islands with penguins, 1995.

With Angel, 2000 (Norman Lono/NYT Pictures).

With Charles Bronfman, "birthright israel" event, Israel, 2000.

"birthright israel" group at Western Wall, 2000.

and Lorillard. In addition, as the Chairman of the Board of Trustees of New York University, he agreed to invest some of the school's endowment with us. The caveat, however, was that Larry did not want to be the sole investor, so we continued in our otherwise unsuccessful fund-raising endeavor. Eventually, in large part because of Larry's support, we launched Institutional Partners, LP, with $12 million. We had reached our monetary goal but we had not been as successful as we had hoped in raising money from endowments.

Then one day, John Levin read an article in the *Wall Street Journal* about The Common Fund, an organization created in the early 1970s to manage money exclusively for school endowments. One of the money managers mentioned as running money for the fund was a friend of John's: Joe McNay of Essex Management in Boston. John called him and asked for an introduction to George Keane, president of The Common Fund. Knowing the Fund's investment style, Joe replied, "Absolutely not. George Keane will never do anything like this."

John said, "Okay, Joe. Then can I call George and say that Joe McNay thinks this is a ridiculous idea for you to even consider talking about?"

Joe said, "That's fine with me."

As a long shot, John put in a call to George Keane. For some reason, George was intrigued by an investment that was "not recommended" for his fine institution. He agreed to meet with John and, eventually, he met with me. Maybe because we were of similar mind and body shape, we really clicked. George asked me to give a presentation to his board of trustees—a whole new experience for me. Surprisingly, and because of strong support from one trustee—Robert Salomon, a partner at Salomon Brothers—The Common Fund agreed to invest. This was the stamp of approval we were waiting for.

In time, we attracted an elite group of blue-chip investors: the World Bank, Carnegie Corporation, Yale University, Duke

University, the University of Minnesota, and others. Within two years, the fund was about $100 million. Eventually, it grew to over $1 billion. Today, allocating to hedge funds is a common practice for endowments and foundations. Back then, it was a huge breakthrough and a rewarding experience.

∞

Running institutional money had one corollary: dealing with the committees of fiduciaries to whom I had a certain reporting responsibility. Periodically, I had to make presentations to the investment committees of the various institutions that had money in our funds. This was one of my least favorite activities. I usually dreaded these unavoidable presentations. I remember one meeting with the investment committee of Yale University. Happily, the meeting was in New York rather than New Haven. I was surrounded by a distinguished group of trustees in a very prestigious law office.

To date, I had been Yale's most successful money manager. They were quite appreciative of my performance. In my presentation, I focused, as I usually did, on macro perceptions. I tended to wax more than a bit philosophic as to the uncertainties I saw in my worldview. Could the economy continue growing at this pace? Were the values of the 1980s sustainable? Would this materialist euphoria allow for sound world leadership? I raised as many questions as I answered.

I felt that the committee had found the presentation provocative and interesting, even though it went beyond the half-hour or so for which it had been scheduled. When it was over, I sensed a general appreciation and left feeling quite satisfied. I heard later that, after I had left, Bart Giamatti, then President of Yale, looked at the group and said, "I had no idea we had Hamlet running our money."

# 10

# MENAGERIES AND MOVIES

F MY POSSESSIONS, THE ONLY ONE THAT I HAVE a deep emotional attachment to is our home in Bedford. It is here that I first learned about and developed a passion for horticulture. Among our reasons for buying the property: the former owner cultivated fruit trees, various berries, and grape vines. I soon became interested in growing berries and, with characteristic intensity, set out to grow every edible berry I could find. We grew red, purple, golden, and black raspberries. Gooseberries of various degrees of tartness were planted as well as *fraise du bois;* blueberries; mulberries; blackberries; jostaberries; black, white, and red currants; huckleberries; and cranberries. If I could find it in a catalog, we grew it. Judy, my mother, my kids, and I also began making jam. Since I was constantly obsessed with weight problems, we tried to avoid the vast amounts of sugar typically used to preserve it. I think we still have some 1980 vintage jam stored away. I do not think it improves with age.

Before long, we added more grapevines, shifting to *vinefera* grapes, which dominate the commercial wine industry. We bought storage equipment, crushers, and whatever else we needed to become a small-time winery. We even had the daughter of a good friend create a beautiful label for our bottles. I used to say that our wine was comparable to that of the Rothschilds, at least in one respect: It cost as much to make. Aside from that, it was not going to win any awards. We eventually stopped wine production and started growing more seedless table grapes. The winemaking equipment was then used for our biannual cider party, for which we made hundreds of gallons of delicious cider from our own apples and pears.

Growing apples and other fruit provides a near year-round pleasure for me. The blossoms in the spring, the sight of tens of trees with ripe fruit, and, ultimately, the variant tastes are a joy to this boy from Brooklyn. With 120 or so trees, there were 70 or 80 different varieties of apples. Some were tart; some sweet; some pink, red, and yellow fleshed. Savoring this common fruit in all its varieties became for me analogous to wine tasting. After a time, I could, blindfolded, identify most of the many varieties by their scent, size, shape, and taste. I love walking through the orchard and looking at colors that range from almost black to light yellow, and sizes that range from two or more pounds to the weight of a large cherry.

In the many flower beds on the property, I have found tremendous pleasure in experimenting with new plants. When I become focused on a particular species, I sometimes lose all sense of proportion. In one year, I bought and had planted over 500 hemerocallis (daylilies). I became enamored of yellow-blossomed magnolias; we now have over 20 different varieties. Perhaps analogous to markets, I love taking risks with marginally hardy plants. Thus, we have planted a large number of camellias, sarracenia, commonly known as pitcherplant, and a range of tender perennials usually from the Northwest that have yet to make it through a New York winter. However, we have been successful with some cacti apricot and white peach trees, prunis mums, and some ladyslippers. I find little in life as pleasurable as learning about new plants from catalogs and nursery owners who have created their own hybrids. There is nothing I look forward to more than a morning walk in the early spring, when the masses of blue crocus dominate our entrance. I welcome the annual display of wildflowers our landscaper, Jerome Rocherolle, orchestrates every year. In most other areas of my life, it does not fit my personality to be patient and uniformly enthusiastic. In our garden, I have managed to be both.

Although I have planted few of the trees, shrubs, and plants myself, I have devoted great effort to becoming horticulturally knowledgeable. Indeed, for some years now, I have read nursery catalogs, including the most obscure and sophisticated, before going to bed at night. The imagery created in catalogs' plant descriptions has a purity of vision that invariably exceeds the reality in the field.

We have an almost encyclopedic collection of Japanese maples, and it is a particular thrill to find a new one. Mostly planted as one-year-old whips, these have now grown into beautiful specimens. Nothing is more magnificent than the intensities of color that dominate this garden for two weeks in spring and perhaps three weeks in autumn. The colors seem to radiate above the trees, almost as if generated by the God I do not believe in.

Shortly after purchasing the property, we bought a contiguous parcel, including a house that once belonged to Theodore Dreiser. Before long, we tore the house down but left the stone substructure. Years later, our daughter, Sara, got married in this "ruin." Dreiser had called his home *Iroki*–Japanese for Garden of Pleasant Surprises. We have continued the name.

The Bedford house is also the site of my extensive zoological collection, which gives me endless pleasure. This evolved from a desire to fill our largest pond with ducks. That collection ended up containing, at one point, most species of waterfowl in existence today. From waterfowl, we continued the collection with guinea hens, turkeys, and barn owls. We have several species of cranes, including East and West African crown cranes, Damoiselles from Northern Europe, and Sarus cranes, the largest in existence. I particularly enjoy dancing with Martha, a Blue crane (the national bird of South Africa). Martha, who is pinioned, jumps several feet in the air as she and I circle each other in our well-choreographed ballet.

Over the years, the menagerie has expanded beyond birds to include all sorts of creatures, large and small. Our first mammal was a Vietnamese pond deer, a *montjac*. Sicilian donkeys, kangaroos, spider monkeys, llamas, alpacas, and zebras followed. Our collection began to leave the realm of reason when we added a range of unusual mammals, including wallabies, capybara, binderong, lemurs, caracal cats, and African crown porcupines. Lately, we have been thinking about three-toed sloths and miniature skunks.

With some of the animals, a personal relationship develops. A male llama named Angel allows me, but no one else, to kiss him. Seeing a baby albino wallabie stick its head out of its mother's pouch is a sight that invariably excites children. Sometimes, the fecundity of certain animals creates its own set of problems. Thus, we have too many zebras, alpacas, and capybaras for which there are no ready homes. We fortunately managed to find a home for our growing herd of rather large African watusi cattle at a friend's farm in upstate Millbrook.

Recently, I was distraught when a camel bit one of my guests on the arm. Naturally, I was initially concerned about my guest's discomfort and tended to that immediately at Northern Westchester Hospital. The abrasion to my guest was, in fact, minor, but because a camel cannot receive rabies shots, the animal had to be put down in order to test his brain for the presence of the disease. He tested negative, but it was too late. Every time I see the mother and baby camel, it saddens me greatly to think about what we had to do.

⟨∞⟩

Animals never cease to amaze me and have been a great source of pleasure for my family and guests. In 1990, I held a meeting of leading Israeli economic figures at my home in Bedford. The purpose of the gathering was to discuss the problems resulting from the massive immigration of Russian Jews into Israel as the Soviet Union collapsed. Because the Israeli economy was not able to employ so many immigrants, unemployment, always a problem, increased significantly. I had developed some ideas on how to deal with this problem, so, through my extensive contacts, I suggested an informal meeting with Israel's economic elite. This meeting included the senior members of the Ministry of Finance, including then Finance Minister Beiga Shohat, as well as the ambassador to the United States. It also included some business leaders and friends: Lester Crown, CEO of General Dynamics; Leonard Garment, a former legal adviser to President Nixon; and, because of his expertise in municipal finance, Richard Ravitch, former head of the Metropolitan Transit Authority. At this gathering, we discussed the development of new infrastructure programs for Israel as a way to create jobs. The programs would include new roads, port facilities, tunnels, subways, rapid transit, and anything else we could think of that would both modernize Israel and help employ the new immigrants.

After a morning of stimulating discussions, we broke for lunch. Judy had prepared a feast of smoked fish and fresh vegetables from our garden, which the Israelis particularly seemed to enjoy. Afterward, I was asked to give a tour of the property. Upon seeing my extensive menagerie and the obvious pleasure I took in each animal, my Israeli guests impressed on me the importance of purchasing a Thai elephant for the Jerusalem Zoo. How could I refuse? She has been named Michaela.

There were about 20 of us, mostly speaking Hebrew, and as we walked toward the bird preserve, I explained that I would show them a special bird. I said that I had a Cereopsis hen that understood—in fact, that spoke—Hebrew. They looked at me dubiously, but I insisted.

As we walked into the preserve, I spotted the goose and pointed her out to Minister Shohat. He ventured some Hebrew and the goose came running over, shaking her chartreuse beak up and down persuasively. The goose then uttered some guttural sounds that, for the uninitiated, could almost pass for Hebrew. Of course, she would do the same for anybody speaking any language. Ultimately, nothing came of this infrastructure summit, but I am certain that, to this day, there are people in Jerusalem still talking about my goose that speaks Hebrew.

∞

Most of the wildfowl I acquired over the years were bought from Michael Lubbock, perhaps the world's most respected bird breeder. Before moving to North Carolina, Mike was head of the United Kingdom's Wildfowl and Wetlands Trust. One of the most enjoyable experiences in Bedford occurs every so often when he arrives with a group of new birds. It is such fun to watch the release of these relatively exotic creatures that I often invite guests, particularly with children, to share in the excitement. During one such visit, Mike told me of the possible availability of two pristine islands in the Falklands archipelago in the South Atlantic. Grand and Steeple Jason Islands are the world's largest nesting area for the black-browed albatross, as well as the home of three different species of penguins and many other unusual creatures. These islands are among the most prized, relatively undisturbed natural habitats in existence today. The islands were for sale because their owner ran afoul of Falkland conservation regulations when he surreptitiously smuggled penguin eggs from these islands to his commercial bird facility in the Cotswolds in England.

It took me longer than Margaret Thatcher to find the Falklands on the map. They are truly distinguished by their remoteness. Nonetheless, Mike Lubbock's description, and the idea of doing my part to preserve the natural habitat of this special place intrigued me. With the help of my good friend David Blackburn, a lawyer from London, I soon made an offer to buy the islands. After considerable negotiation involving both the seller and the Falkland Islands authorities, the deal was done.

Judy and I, along with our animal keeper, Joe Daddona, David Blackburn, Michael and Ali Lubbock, and Frank Todd, a noted ornithologist, went to visit the islands soon thereafter. It was not easy to get there. We flew from Punta Arenas, Chile, to Stanley in the Falklands, on a once-a-week flight that took six hours on a plane with no bathroom. When we arrived in Stanley, the governor treated us to a "state" dinner. The next day, the British military offered us the use of two large helicopters for the one-hour flight to my newly acquired islands.

When we stepped off the helicopter, we found that the island was covered with thick green vegetation and, in some places, had a remarkable tropical-like tussock grass, which was over six feet tall. There were no trees, however. Walking along, we soon came upon the albatrosses. There were birds as far as the eye could see—thousands upon thousands of eight-pound, two-month-old chicks awaiting the return of their parents, who were scouring the seas for their dinner.

Most of the creatures on the islands were unguardedly friendly because they were unaccustomed to human contact. We walked among the groups of penguins, and they were unafraid and as curious about us as we were about them. Some even came up and nibbled on our shoes. Particularly amusing was the Johnny Rook, a small predator that would blatantly attack us, often aiming for the top of our heads with considerable success. We spent about half a day on the islands. When it was time to leave, we found the helicopter propellers totally populated by Johnny Rooks. To get them off the helicopters, we had to throw them ample chunks of raw meat so that we could start the motors.

Observing this wildlife refuge firsthand, I felt that Judy and I had done our share to ensure that these engaging creatures are safe, and that the marine habitats and resources on which they depend are not threatened. To ensure that these remarkable islands remain an ecological refuge, we have recently gifted them to the Wildlife Conservation Society with great confidence that they will protect them in perpetuity.

Some of the birds that we keep in Bedford are native to the South Atlantic and the Jason Islands. One bird, called the Falkland Flightless Steamer Duck, was the single most aggressive creature ever to inhabit our grounds in Bedford. The male steamer duck, with no provocation, would chase almost anyone who came within a few feet and viciously bite anyone within his reach. The bird brought out my mischievous nature: I often set up guests to venture just close enough to ensure a chase.

∞

About 20 years ago, Judy and I began collecting art even though, for some time, I had harbored a cynical view of collecting and collectors. I sensed that many so-called art devotees had a shallow knowledge base and a superficial commitment to collecting. I determined that if I were going to collect, I would seek purity and depth of knowledge, as idealistic as that might be.

Despite these misgivings, Judy and I began buying art. It soon became a near overriding passion. A very early purchase was a watercolor by Paul Klee, an artist whom we appreciate for his wit, provocation, and thorough inventiveness. In particular, I love his sense of humor, some of which still escapes me. Over the years, and largely through Judy's stewardship, we have developed a fine collection of works on paper that includes, among others, Cézanne, Schiele, Picasso, Klee, Matisse, Pollack, and de Kooning. We also purchased a number of Seurat conté crayon drawings for their evocative elegance.

While we have some fine paintings by Gauguin, Chagall, and Dix, I react more readily to our drawings, which, to my eye, reveal more of the artist's sensibility, creating a freshness accentuated by its fragility.

I seem to opt for social commentary in many of my choices. One such work is a recently acquired Goya drawing in which every stroke evokes meaning even more subtly than in his powerful notebook, *Disasters of War.* My very first purchase at age 25 was a double-sided ink drawing by George Grosz from the late 1920s depicting a Prussian officer, a capitalist, and a religious fanatic anticipating the problems soon to come for Germany. We are now almost out of wall space in our apartment but that does not impinge on our enthusiasm.

One of the most special moments in our collecting was our recent gift of Rembrandt's *The Apostle Peter Kneeling,* 1631, which became Israel's first Rembrandt. Oddly, I derived greater pleasure from giving this Rembrandt—particularly at a depressed time in Israel—than I felt from owning it ourselves.

Our collection has also grown to include Judaica, ancient art, and Peruvian feathered textiles. I was drawn to collecting Judaica not so much because of the aesthetics, but because of my continuing effort to resolve my conflicted thoughts on the issue of faith. Over time I have been able to appreciate the beauty of many of these ceremonial objects mostly from lost European communities. Seeing and holding the historic precious objects of our religion, which had been used by generations of my ancestors, gave me a special feeling. I close my eyes and envisage the centuries-old synagogues and Jewish homes in which these were objects of pride. This feeling of somehow being a link in the Jewish chain exceeds the actual aesthetics of the pieces.

One day, years ago, in Jerusalem, I decided that I would begin collecting *tzedakah* (charity) boxes as the main focus of my Judaica collection. I chose them because they represent that special Jewish value of providing for society's weakest members. I scoured all the Judaica and antique shops I could find and made purchases conditioned on authenticity. I then brought twelve of these objects to the curator of the Israel Museum who, after carefully examining them, informed me that none was authentic. Some were modern copies. Some were pastiches and some were old, but not Jewish.

I persisted, however, and, over time, I amassed a very large collection of these boxes. Again, years later, I submitted them to an expert appraisal and discovered that perhaps a third of these were also not authentic. This is the risk that comes with being a new collector, and even a not-so-new collector, in an area where dealers are not always paragons of virtue.

Still, I now have an extensive and comprehensive collection of Judaica that, peculiarly, also includes anti-Semitic objects such as wooden toys that caricature religious Jews with humped backs and long noses as well as more subtle cartoons from nineteenth-century English publications.

The area of collecting that I find most rewarding is ancient art. Through objects that, in many instances, are older than the Bible, one captures tangible elements of the history of humanity and its civilizations in ways that provoke the imagination.

Seeing archaic Greek vase paintings, or a marble sculpture that, 2,500 years later, is still profoundly appealing to contemporary humans, inspires me in ways that history books cannot. Nevertheless, my collections' beauty is not always readily obvious. After I showed a portion of my ancient Middle Eastern material, particularly bronze statuettes, to a business associate, he assured me that I need not worry about their being vulnerable to theft because if offered on the street, there would probably be no takers.

My motivation in collecting these pieces has been overwhelmingly visual, which might justify my lack of devotion to becoming fully cognizant of and knowledgeable about the cultures in which this art was created. For some collectors, my approach may be insufficient. Indeed, I sometimes chastise myself because I feel inadequate. I am challenged to learn more although I have often, using stock market parlance, invested before I investigated.

Ironically, one ancient-object, which I purchased innocently after museum inquiry, resulted in my greatest fiasco. In 1991, I acquired a *phiale,* a gold ceremonial plate of Greek origin presumably dating to the fourth century B.C. I bought the object through a New York antiquities dealer who claimed to have located it through an Italian coin dealer. Because gold is a malleable metal readily subject to forgery, before purchasing the *phiale,* I brought it to the conservation department of the Metropolitan Museum of Art where it was studied by both curators and conservators for well over one month. The museum had its own *phiale,* nearly identical to this one, which had been prominently displayed for many years. Thus, the museum experts were anxious to compare the two objects, particularly to help determine the authenticity of both plates. After concluding their analysis, they said to me, perhaps a bit hesitantly, "Yours is as authentic as ours is."

Oddly perhaps, I was comforted by their judgment and purchased the *phiale* for more than $1 million. It was prominently displayed in my New York living room for several years. Then, one day, the Customs Department of the U.S. Treasury appeared, unannounced, search warrant in hand, and confiscated it. They were acting on behalf of the Italian government, which claimed that the plate had been illegally exported, violating Italian law restricting the trade in ancient objects of value that were part of their national patrimony.

News of the confiscation quickly spread through the art world because of the U.S. authorities' seeming departure from their usual practice by choosing to enforce a foreign country's patrimony laws. The implications became far reaching. Many museums focused on this issue as the case grew more and more byzantine. In fact, a group of prestigious U.S. museums submitted an amicus brief in support of the *phiale's* return to me.

I lost the initial judgment and two subsequent appeals, and the United States Supreme Court declined to hear the case. This failed legal battle cost an additional $1 million. While it was incontrovertible that the loss and the subsequent legal cost should have been the dealer's responsibility, he pled poverty. After a certain point, the case became a mission for me. Not only because of the injustice I had experienced but, more importantly, because I was inadvertently representing the world's cultural institutions, which are increasingly being attacked for the "questionable" provenance of some of their works of art.

This story is not yet over, both in a micro and a macro sense. As far as the *phiale* is concerned, there is an ongoing trial in Italy of the Italian dealer who sold it. He now claims the *phiale* is a modern fake. On the macro level, the controversy over national patrimony grows and is perhaps the dominant contemporary issue in the world of art today. From my perspective, this has been a costly education and, even worse, I am not sure I could avoid the same mistake again. In stock market terms, I have lost 100 percent of my investment times two. Even I cannot do that too often.

∞

In the mid-1980s, I got into the movie business. My involvement began innocently enough. I received a phone call from Teddy Kollek, then the mayor of Jerusalem. He asked me if I would help his son, Amos, complete the financing of a film that was well along toward release. I did not know Amos, but he needed $40,000 to finish the editing and postproduction of a project ultimately titled *Goodbye, New York*. I loaned him the money as a favor to Teddy, whom I deeply admire. I must admit I was also intrigued by the film business and the opportunity to participate in a field that, from a distance, seemed so glamorous.

Over the years, the movie business seemed to lure many Wall Streeters for varying reasons, but rarely led to bottom-line success. I too was to follow this unprofitable path. As a teenager, I had taken special subway trips into Manhattan to see art films that would not play in Brooklyn. Because of my financial success I was now able to enter a business that had always held a special place in my heart and mind.

*Goodbye, New York,* for which I was given a credit as executive producer (a dubious description), starred Julie Hagerty and a variety of Israeli actors, as well as Amos Kollek himself. The film concerned a Christian girl who broke up with her boyfriend in New York and then boarded a plane to Paris. She wore a big black hat, which she pulled down over her head. Her black hat, when viewed from a certain angle, looked the same as the black hats of some Hasidim, who were sitting near her on the plane. The flight attendants, assuming she was part of the contingent of Hasidim heading for Israel, did not wake her when the plane stopped in Paris on its way to Tel Aviv. She woke up when the plane landed in Israel. The film traced her trip through Israel, much of which was funny because of all the weird characters she met along the way.

When the film opened in New York in 1985, it received good reviews and became a commercial hit. It played at one of the Embassy theaters for a record number of weeks. Indeed, *Goodbye, New York* was so successful that Amos made a bit of money from it and paid back the full amount he had borrowed. Financially, this would be my greatest motion picture success. I should have learned then that even a box office success does not assure profitability for an independently made film.

After *Goodbye, New York,* I financed several more films with Amos. The last one I was deeply involved in starred Faye Dunaway. Titled *Double Edge,* and released in 1991, it was based on the outbreak of the first Intifada—the Palestinian revolt against the Israelis, a civil insurrection of kids throwing rocks and bombs.

At this time, on television, particularly on CNN, Arab kids were often portrayed like David facing the Goliath-like Israeli soldiers. Troops in armor would be shown shooting at these kids with rubber bullets, or worse. I thought it would be worthwhile to counter the negative publicity heaped on Israel by making a film that provided a more balanced view of the complexities of the politics of the Middle East. I discussed this idea with Amos, and he wrote a screenplay that was made into a worthwhile film. We lost every penny of the $1.7 million we sank into it (mostly mine), but I thought the final film was quite decent.

Indeed, I still think *Double Edge* is an exciting movie. It is a work of cinema verité that has, as a concept, an American reporter (Dunaway) on temporary assignment in Jerusalem where she is, for personal reasons, anxious to make a name for herself in a very short period of time. (The working title of the script was "Three Weeks in Jerusalem.") Using this fictional format, we created cinema verité interviews with real people—among them, Abba Eban, Rabbi Meir Kahane, Teddy Kollek, Hanan Ashrawi, and a whole range of ordinary people, including parents whose children had been killed in the conflict. That was the background for the story, which centers on the heroine's getting involved with an Arab terrorist. Shot entirely in Israel, *Double Edge* received moderately good reviews, but, as usual, it was a commercial disaster.

I also got to make my acting debut in two of Amos's movies. In his 1989 epic, *Highstakes,* I appeared for less than 30 seconds as a character soliciting a prostitute. This was topped by my next appearance in the classic *Forever Lulu* in which I triumphed for a whole minute as a ticket-taker.

Although none of our films was profitable, I remain quite fond of Amos. I have since loaned him modest sums, and he has since made some highly acclaimed films. Although I was not involved in the productions, their success has gratified me. I particularly admire the way he always casts beautiful blondes to play opposite the character he plays. All in a day's work in the movie business. *Double Edge* was the last film I made with Amos.

Along with a partner, Tom Baer, I then started financing films made by Orion Pictures. Eventually, this company went bankrupt, but before it did, our Orion projects included financing the scripts for the successful *Addams Family* and for *Married to It,* with Cybill Shepherd and Ron Silver. In these projects, I was involved only on the money side.

The most successful and prestigious movie in which I was an investor was a documentary called *Hotel Terminus,* about Klaus Barbie, the Nazi "Butcher of Lyons." It won the Academy Award for Best Foreign Documentary. It was a critical success but the extent of its financial success was limited. At least I managed to break even.

Judy and I once visited the set of a movie Tom and I were making in Toronto. Frankly, I did not enjoy seeing how slowly and expensively a movie set works. It is like watching grass grow at $300,000 a day. Also, at Tom's suggestion, we invested in October Films, but, once again, we managed, with a great deal of effort, to only break even. I must confess to a continuing love of movie making and to an absolute conviction that I will never make a penny at it. I live in the hope that someday I will be proven wrong and a movie will finally yield a profit. Even I grow tired of constantly asking my movie partners the same question: "Where is my money?"

# II

# THE CRASH OF 1987

N 1987, I REGARDED MYSELF AS BOTH A GENIUS and a fool. Early in the year, I foresaw a coming crash, but once I identified the approaching disaster, I did not remain true to my convictions. I succumbed to the reigning complacency and the pressure created by our underperforming the averages for a few months. In the end, I was hurt as badly by the crash as any rank amateur— only, for me, it was worse.

In April 1987, six months before the crash, I wrote the following to my investors:

> Of course, the market can go higher, materially higher. But, to the traditional investor (for better or worse, I probably qualify), there are a number of warning signs in today's market. Relative to historical norms, price/earnings ratios are extended and dividend yields are low. Few values jump out at you. Perhaps more important, it is hard to imagine a continuation of the low growth, low inflation, low interest rate environment indefinitely. Either the economy will weaken or, if it picks up, interest rates will likely rise. In this circumstance, while continued monetary accommodation and, for that matter, continuation of the trend for buyouts and buybacks provide support for the market, downside risk seems substantial. With the advent of so-called "program trading" and the proliferation of new, derivative instruments, potential volatility has been greatly increased. Fifty- or even

one-hundred-point daily moves of the Dow Jones Industrials should no longer be considered shocking.

Prescient, yet I would not benefit from my own advice. I continued:

> I am inclined to be far more cautious in these circumstances despite the obvious risk, given the current momentum in the market, of missing a further substantial rise in stock prices. It has always been my intent to invest the partnership's money as if it were my own. Therefore, I have always sought opportunities where the downside risk seems manageable. This is not the case now, in my judgment, in the U.S. stock market. In sum, our cautious attitude will result in less exposure; therefore, we will continue to underperform a strong market.

Looking back, I can see how the letter—composed not so long before the crash—is prophetic. But six months is a long time, especially in the investment business, and the fervor I expressed so fully in that letter did not last. Within months, I was net long again. I had concluded that the risk of being out of the market was greater than the risk of being in, so we bought stocks in an expensive, exuberant market. There is a certain virtue in measuring one's performance annually; there is also a risk of being led down the path of temptation, which comes in many guises. Sometimes, the immediacy of opportunity—the attraction of individual stocks—precluded concerns about overvaluation. We got long and we made money, so we got longer and it seemed easy. In retrospect, it was too easy.

By the end of August, the funds were up around 35 percent and we were feeling quite good about the year—and about most of our individual stocks. For each position, there was an enthusiastic analyst, and the analysts' convictions held sway. The market seemed tired toward the end of the summer, but I was not overly sensitive to it. Each day, however, I would reflect on one question: What would eventually make this overpriced market go down? The perplexing dilemma was: Although the market was overvalued by most historic standards, it seemed we might be entering a new era. Could this be a period of secular earnings' multiple expansion? The supply of and the demand for stocks were unusually positive and were aided by Americans' growing comfort with the use of leverage, which may have been a precursor of the extraordinary stock market of the 1990s.

Through September, the market became erratic, but we did not reduce our net long exposure. Comfortable with the specifics of our portfolio, we were meaningfully exposed on the long side. By the end of the summer, the year's performance was shaping up quite well, but when the market crash came in October, we were unprepared. The foreboding in my letter was correct, but, in the end, temptation won out. The day of reckoning had arrived.

❦

On the Friday before the crash, the market had been down more than 100 points. Blocks of stock were trading at unusually steep discounts, which naturally created some concern. I called a staff meeting in the afternoon and asked whether anyone had any insights as to what had changed. Was there something in the macro world that I was missing? I could not get clarity from the meeting and perhaps I was not as wary as I should have been. Even over the weekend, the fear that was in the air and the press largely escaped me.

On Monday morning, stocks opened dramatically lower again. By 10:30 A.M., the Dow Jones Industrial Average was down more than 120 points and the news services were already calling it widespread investor panic. By midday, with the Dow down close to 200 points, and feeling that perhaps it was oversold and we had seen the lows, I began to buy Standard & Poor's (S&P) futures, which were now trading at a substantial discount. As an extraordinarily active trader in S&P futures, I was experienced in "reading" the significance of premiums and discounts. Futures were now trading at a compelling discount to their underlying value, which reflected an already substantially dislocated market.

I entered buy orders on my usual scale-down basis: "Buy 10 S&Ps every 10 ticks."

As the market's decline picked up, orders were being executed far more quickly than I had expected. In a short time, I closed out my short in S&P futures, which had been a hedge to my net long stock position. I kept on buying. With the market down 250 points, I was now both net long stocks and long S&P futures. For a fleeting moment, I was encouraged as the market began to stabilize down 250 points and started a gentle rebound. In the course of the next hour or so, it rallied from down 250 to down 200 to down 100. I started to think that, being a savvy trader, I might have picked the bottom.

As the afternoon wore on, it became evident that the market would again test the lows. By two o'clock, it was again falling. By three o'clock, it was falling faster: down 300, then down 350. A sense of panic was spreading. The news ticker announced that President Ronald Reagan would make a statement about the market after the close. At this point, I knew we were really on new ground. We sat in the trading room and watched the free fall: down 450.

By the closing bell, the size of the market's loss numbed me. The Dow was down 508 points—a 22 percent decline, and the single worst day in the stock market since the Great Depression. I was still trying to get a grasp on what the market was saying, but I could not figure it out. Nothing seemed changed fundamentally in the world, but the market fell apart. Maybe one sees profound change only in retrospect. Sitting at my desk at the end of the day, I realized, perhaps for the very first time, that the market had actually crashed.

We stayed in the office that Monday until midnight. Late in the evening, I decided I had the courage to be a buyer of S&P futures again on Tuesday. I thought the market had declined so far and so fast that it would have to rebound.

To make matters worse, early the next morning, before the market opened, I received an upsetting call from Morgan Stanley, the clearing broker for our futures trading. Morgan Stanley was raising the margin requirements on our futures account. This was distressing news because we were now largely invested, leveraged, and planning on buying more futures. Given the precarious state of the market, Morgan Stanley opted to reduce its credit exposure to our firm and to some of its other hedge fund "speculators." If we did not raise sufficient cash to meet the new margin call by the end of the market's close that day, Morgan Stanley would begin liquidating our account.

I was furious and immediately put in a call to Bob Mnuchin, who ran the equities division at Goldman Sachs. Always cool under pressure, Bob assured me that, after checking with the Management Committee, Goldman, our prime broker since inception, would be content with our creditworthiness for futures trading. I immediately moved all of our futures clearing to Goldman Sachs. We did not trade with Morgan Stanley again for years.

∝∾

Over the years, I have tried to forget the actual dollar amount that I lost on Black Monday and the days afterward. But I do know that, in September 1987, Steinhardt Partners was up by about 45 percent, and by the end of the calendar year, we were up only 4 percent. We lost nearly the entire year's profit on the day of the crash and the few days that followed. As always, during periods when we were losing money, I significantly reduced our overall exposure and raised cash. Therefore, when the market finally bounced back, I was underexposed and was slow to make the money back.

I was so depressed that fall that I did not want to go on. I took the crash personally. The issue of timing haunted me. My prescient forewarnings earlier in the year made the losses all the more painful. Maybe I was losing my judgment. Maybe I just was not as good as I used to be. My confidence was shaken. I felt alone. My instinct had told me to be cautious with the market, but I had invested as though I were an inexperienced mutual-fund bull, simply putting money to work in the market. So much for variant perception!

The stock market crash dominated the media for weeks. Journalists suggested that we were living through a special moment in financial history, but I was too close to have such a perspective. Until this point, I had always outperformed in down markets—sometimes, spectacularly. Now I had failed, and my failure gnawed at me. I canceled vacation plans. I was miserable.

"We had maintained a cautious stance toward the market for a number of months," I wrote to my investors on October 26, a week after the crash, "believing that the combination of rising interest rates and indecisiveness among policy makers in Washington had created circumstances in which it would be hard for stocks to rise further. However, we by no means anticipated the violent and enormous decline that occurred in the past two weeks." Even this was an understatement.

⬧

In retrospect, the Crash of 1987 predicted nothing. A bear market did not follow it. There was a panic—a short, swift, compressed decline. Perhaps the market had gone up too fast at the same time that bond yields had become very competitive. People looked for nuance in interest rates and political statements to create meaning where none was obvious. Most believed that the stock market was a reliable indicator of future change, and its message seemed clear. The world went to great lengths to create a rationale for the crash. Would a recession follow? A depression? Political turmoil? Nothing?

There was no economic justification for the market's collapse. Indeed, the overall economy showed a real resilience. Instead of being a harbinger of economic weakness or some dread financial crisis, the crash was overwhelmingly a phenomenon of the market's internal inability to adjust to the vastly increased volume and the new products created during the 1970s and 1980s, when efficient market theories had abounded on Wall Street. Highly quantitative academics had become the new gurus of financial markets by creating a host of portfolio management tools designed to limit losses and control relative risk in markets. Portfolio insurance and program trading created new computer-based techniques for continuously buying baskets of stocks as markets rose, or, as in this period, selling as markets declined. These products had been tested and used successfully during "normal" markets but never during the dramatic price declines witnessed during these few days. The discontinuity of prices and the constant selling of these "insured" portfolios exacerbated the market's crash in an unprecedented way. Ironically, the one time when investors most needed their portfolio insurance to limit losses, it failed them miserably.

Furthermore, there had been a reduction in the importance of the "old" stability creators, including the New York Stock Exchange specialist system. Also, during the crash, there had been a tremendous disparity in the performance of different specialist firms. Moreover, the upstairs proprietary trading desks of the major brokerage firms played a lesser role in stabilizing markets because their capital had shrunk relative to the increased size of the overall market. In addition, there had been a major shift from retail to institutional dominance. Finally, the significantly increased volume had exacerbated the debacle. For example, the tape was running so late that people had no idea how low or at what prices most stocks were trading.

A slew of studies were conducted by the New York Stock Exchange (NYSE), the Securities and Exchange Commission (SEC), Congress, and a Presidential Task Force to investigate the circumstances of the crash. They all basically reached the same, not so profound, conclusion: There had been a bull market before the crash, and all bull markets sooner or later come to an end. It is as natural for markets to go down as to go up, but human nature does not easily accept the misery that usually accompanies declines without at least seeking a rationale.

As a result of those investigations, there were new constraints and limits on movements up and down in the market—a belated recognition of all that had changed. Even then, the severity of the stock market decline was assumed to be a harbinger of an impending fiasco: a looming recession, rising interest rates, and problems resulting from a monetary dispute between the Federal Reserve and the Bundesbank. None of this happened. In the end, few economic lessons were to be gleaned from the Crash of 1987. Financial history does not always repeat itself.

◌

When it rains, it pours. As if enough had not already gone wrong in the portfolio in October 1987, an annoying sideline was the debacle in our convertible arbitrage portfolio. In 1986, I had hired a portfolio manager who specialized in convertibles. Convertible bonds are hybrid instruments that have a fixed-income component and an equity option. In convertible arbitrage, one buys a convertible bond and hedges the risk by simultaneously shorting the underlying stock. Done properly, this kind of arbitrage is low risk and has low correlation to the equity markets. The key is getting the hedge ratio correct so that, in times of stress in the stock market, the value of the bond portfolio will hold up relative to the decline in the equity component. This requires owning bonds of reasonable quality that will not decline as much as the underlying stock in a bear market.

In the profit and loss (P&L) statement in the days immediately following the crash, I was relieved to see that our convertible portfolio, while small, had indeed performed even better than I could have hoped for. The P&L for converts showed that we were up about 10 percent for the month of October. At least one part of our portfolio had survived the crash. Then, I began to wonder. As a routine check, I asked one of my traders to reconfirm that all the "marks" used by the portfolio manager on these mostly over-the-counter convertibles were in fact correct. The next day, I received another blow. The bonds had been mismarked. They were of poor quality and had failed to achieve any independent bond value or protection. The "low-risk" portfolio was down as much as the rest of the market (about 30 percent), not up. This created the only monthly downward P&L revision in the history of our firm.

My rage was uncontrollable. The shouting emanating from my office reached a new decibel level. When the portfolio manager finally had the courage to mutter a few words back to me, he said, "All I want to do is kill myself." I replied coolly, "Can I watch?"

❧

At the end of October, at the annual American Friends of the Israel Museum gala at Lincoln Center, which Judy organized, the air was thick with gloom. Everyone showed up, yet there was only one topic of discussion, the crash. There was laughter and camaraderie, but it was somehow constrained by the knowledge that almost all the people in the room were a lot poorer than they had been one month before.

Having done well in so many market climates, particularly in bear markets, I was miserable at having performed so badly. As usual, people would come to me and ask my views, but my efforts to be cheerful were transparent. Whatever I said did not reflect deep conviction because I did not have any. At the same time, people were intent on listening to my words of "market wisdom." All I could muster was: "The market crashed and in my eyes it portends nothing." I would then add, "But I have been no smarter than anyone else." Perhaps people thought I was being humble, but I knew better. I could not wait to leave the gala, even though it was normally one of my favorite evenings of the year.

❧

The following year, I made a recovery in our funds' performance by going back and focusing on fundamental bottoms-up stock picking. I tried to find the best stocks I could on both the long and short sides. My style invariably was "Four yards up the middle in a cloud of dust" rather than long-gaining heroics. I managed even greater intensity because of my failure in the crash. Over time, I was able to put the disaster into perspective. I came to realize that, in normal periods and in normal markets (both up and down), I had almost never failed to make money. I once calculated the number of months, in all the years I had been in business, in which the funds were profitable versus the number of months in which we had lost. The number of losing months was less than 5 percent of the total. In the final analysis, that was a record I could live with, except during those few months when I was actually losing money. Then my memory of past successes faded. I lost perspective.

❧

A couple of years earlier, an article written about me in *Institutional Investor* had described my keen interest in horticulture.

Included was a caricature of me working in my raspberry patch in Bedford. After reading that article, one of my investors, Louisa Spencer, an adventurous and philanthropic woman, solicited me in early 1987 for a modest contribution to a major capital campaign then under way at the Brooklyn Botanical Gardens, an organization with which she had been actively involved. I agreed to make the gift.

In December 1987, while I was still reeling from my post-crash melancholy, Louisa again called, this time to invite Judy and me to join her on a trip to the Botanical Gardens. I had grown up in Brooklyn, had a passionate interest in horticulture, yet I had never visited the Gardens. So, on a snowy day in the winter of 1987, Judy, Louisa, and I drove to Brooklyn.

When we arrived at the Botanical Gardens, located in the center of the borough of my youth, I immediately found the place fascinating. Louisa, in her particularly charming way, described a dilemma facing the fund-raising project that was already under way. A disagreement with the major donor had made it precariously urgent for the Gardens to find a new substitute. It did not occur to me that I was being targeted to fulfill his pledge.

I kept thinking about the beauty of the Gardens on that snowy day, and how life-affirming a gift to this organization might be. This thought process was driven by my then market-induced depressed state. My inability to separate my performance from my overall sense of self continued to plague me, and I remained unrealistic in my self-appraisal. Yet, that visit was uplifting. Later that week, I called Louisa and asked her for a further explanation of the Gardens' funding needs. Donald Moore, the director of the Gardens, called and provided me with the details that had been worked out previously with the failed donor.

The necessary gift, $3 million, was a multiple of my previous philanthropic giving. Its magnitude made me uncomfortable. Nevertheless, I agreed to make the donation. This was, at that time, the largest gift ever given to a Brooklyn institution. Given my state of mind following the crash, I needed to do something that would make me feel good about myself again. This gift was the perfect antidote, made as it was when I felt both personally and financially insecure. It was a positive act that did as much for my spirit as it did for the Gardens. Subsequently, I have made more sizable contributions to other causes, but this gift had special meaning to me because of its timing. It was a gift to Brooklyn, and it allowed me to feel optimistic once again. For me, the Crash of 1987 and the Steinhardt Conservatory at the Brooklyn Botanical Gardens will always remain inextricably linked. The dedication of the Conservatory would take place exactly one year later, on the anniversary of Black Monday.

We came back from the crash—with a vengeance. In 1988, our funds were up 48 percent. In both 1989 and 1990, they were up 26 percent. With the exception of the 1987 Crash, the decade had been a period of enormous success for our funds. Our consistent high returns far outperformed the Dow Jones Industrials, Standard & Poor's, and the Russell 2000 averages. Continued lower interest rates, coupled with lower inflation and reduced volatility in overall economic activity as the result of the Federal Reserve's constructive policies, formed a doorway to the Golden 1990s. These were truly spectacular years, when I began moving into the macro arena. In 1991, 1992, and 1993, our funds were up approximately 60 percent per year—staggering amounts, even by my standards. Retrospectively, I have a far keener memory of the painful moments of 1987 than I do of the next six years of glorious success. Looking back it is as if they happened naturally, almost without effort. Why is that?

# 12

# THE STEINHARDT STYLE

UR TRACK RECORD OVER THE YEARS WAS achieved through an intense devotion to the principles of long-term investing that was tempered by my compulsive need to have monthly, weekly, and even daily profits. In some years, we did well on the strength of concentrated positions in a few well-chosen stocks. In later years, our equity performance was sometimes dwarfed by directional macro bets. Unlike most money managers, we were almost as comfortable being short stocks as being long, and we usually played both sides aggressively. We started off with a long and impressive record in the stock market and then became a serious participant in the bond market, both domestic and foreign. We irregularly speculated in currencies, and we employed the modern derivative products (options, futures, swaps, and so on) usually as quickly as they were created. Above all, we were flexible, opportunistic, and unconstrained in where we would and could invest.

Ultimately, though, a great deal of our success came from getting the markets' overall direction right. In 1967, when we first started the firm, our strength—given that Howard, Jerry, and I had all of our experience as securities analysts—came from our fundamental stock picking. We had faith in the efficacy of understanding and analyzing individual companies. At this early stage in business, we took the classic hedge fund view that markets are subject to so many variables that direction was nearly impossible to predict. Thus, when we first started off, we did virtually no trading, and almost all serious long positions were held for long-term appreciation. That view did not last too long; I began to realize that adverse market movements could periodically dwarf the impact of even the best stock picking. We remained fundamental stock pickers but the emphasis changed. More often than not, the net exposure of our capital (gross longs minus gross shorts) began to determine our success.

*Instinct* and *intuition* are words used to describe unconscious processes that bear on judgments in a range of human activities. The stock market is an inexact phenomenon: laypersons' opinions often seem as worthy as professionals', and shoeshine men and brokers compete for genius. Thus, the methodology by which one makes judgments is individual and lacks preordained rules. I have frequently pondered why my ability to predict market change, particularly in finite time periods, has been better than most. Market timing is not everything in managing a portfolio, but it always counts and sometimes is the critical variable. Moreover, I soon discovered that I had a natural instinct for trading, and this became a cornerstone of my career.

As far back as 1965, I was betting with a colleague at Loeb Rhodes on daily market direction. We used the Dow Jones Industrial Average and, after the market's close, each wrote down our prediction for the next day. I won 22 days in a row. In my view, this win was not random. At the same time, it was not a reflection of analysis, intelligence, or methodology. Is the word *instinct* appropriate here? I am not sure. Indeed, throughout my career, I maintained unusual confidence in my ability to predict market change.

I have spent much of my career listening to "stories" or pitches from analysts in my firm or from top-ranked research

186

analysts at brokerage houses. Even more narrowly, I received endless opportunities from block traders at the major institutional desks. I inevitably made many judgments based on limited information. Yet, the challenge invariably was to use the sum total of my knowledge and intuition to make the right probability judgments.

Some of the decisions were of a long-term nature; others were unvarnished trades, yet they had the same element of employing an often inchoate judgment. From what were these judgments derived? Is one born with instinct or intuition? Are some people "naturals," like some athletes? I do not think so.

Beginning at a very early age, I have made cumulatively more judgments, and more investment decisions based on the same kinds of data, than almost anyone else. This process unconsciously leads to a sharpening, a fine tuning, that, over time, results in fewer mistakes. In this repetitious behavior, a learning occurs that is not consciously understandable but allows one to ferret out the higher probability from the lower. Thus, one develops "good instincts." Often listening to an idea led me to an entirely different conclusion than the proponent of that same idea, whose knowledge was far deeper than mine. It seemed knowledge was necessary but insufficient. While I have certainly made my fair share of mistakes, the filtering process that I contributed was extraordinarily effective.

Generally, I tried to look first at the big picture of where the market was going. Then I would find stocks or other instruments to construct a portfolio that reflected my worldview. I would establish a conceptual framework and then look for the specific. My style contrasts with that of bottoms-up stock pickers who focus on company fundamentals regardless of overall market direction. Of course it is too simplistic to dichotomize market approaches between bottoms up and top down, but one invariably has a bias toward one or the other.

Yet, when it came to individual stock selection, my training and the language of my firm leaned toward rigorous fundamental financial analyses, which included myriad statistics, sophisticated and otherwise. There was an intellectual premium for knowing more detail than one's competition, however relevant. The great thrust of our effort was to obtain a long-term understanding of what was happening in both a micro and a macro sense. Sometimes this translated into longer-term holdings and concentration in various stocks and industry groups. Often, however, the results of this work were used in making shorter-term transactions—for example, when a long-term development had an exaggerated short-term impact, or when, for market timing considerations, we adjusted the portfolio to reflect a changed view on market direction.

Thus, there was continuous tension between short-term perceptions and long-term holdings. This tended to create conflict and, at times, harsh disagreement. I was the chief portfolio manager, so my views inevitably dominated—sometimes against the judgments of others. Many times, for example, my market view would dictate reducing the overall long exposure of the portfolio, undermining the extensive work done by my analysts on companies that they felt were undervalued and attractive. Despite the inevitable conflict, I felt that this continuous internal challenging of views was constructive. Others, I am sure, disagreed.

∞

Over the years, I gained a reputation for having an aggressive management style. In retrospect, I would say that my style could be described as combative at times. People said there really were two Michael Steinhardts. One was my five-to-nine personality, which was fairly calm and mellow—some even declared it "charming." This was my demeanor after the markets closed, when I could immediately become objective and distant from the vagaries of the day's action. That was my time to be a devoted family man and perhaps a gracious host, with the help of my wife, Judy. But then there was my other side, my nine-to-five personality: I ruled unconstrained and sometimes ruthlessly. I would be scowling and fuming, shouting over the intercom, storming in and out of the trading room. During those hours, I had little ability to put the market or my performance in perspective.

A highlight of each day was the Profit and Loss (P&L) Statement, the scoreboard. Even if we were having a good day—say, up 2 percent while the market was up 1 percent—instead of being pleased about our gain, I would focus on the stocks in our portfolio that were losing money. Every day, sometimes every hour, when I sensed a problem in the action of a stock, I brought that scrutiny and intensity to each position we held. I had an overriding need to win every day. If I was not winning, I suffered as though a major tragedy had occurred.

It was not in my nature to be good at giving positive reinforcement to my peers. This stemmed from the fact that I was never quite satisfied with my own accomplishments. Instead of praising success, I too often focused on what could have been achieved better.

I remember one time when one of my analysts made a sizable investment in Esmark (ESM), a food service conglomerate. We owned about 350,000 shares of ESM at an average cost of approximately $27 per share. For months, the stock traded in a range between $25 and $29 per share—back and forth, up and down, week after week. The analyst maintained his enthusiasm; he said ESM was undervalued and was the subject of a potential acquisition. I, however, was growing weary of it.

One Friday, the stock had closed at $27. On Monday morning, Aramark announced a $39 bid for the company. The analyst was thrilled. I fully intended to congratulate him, but when I went into his office, the first words out of my mouth were: "Why didn't you buy more of this stock last week? Why did we need to have Esmark in the portfolio all these months when it did nothing?" I am not sure that I was totally serious, but it certainly must have sounded that way.

It was as hard for me to give someone simple praise, even when well deserved, as it was for me to occasionally pat myself on the back. My internalized standard and my competitive intensity were so high that even successes that for most would be considered outstanding did not justify my giving special recognition. Only belatedly did I recognize how tied my performance was to my sense of self, which reinforced how hard driving I could be.

∽

Throughout the market day, I had an open-door policy. Anyone could walk into my office and interrupt at any time. They could discuss any investment. The immediacy of information, a trading opportunity, or a change of view on any position in the portfolio took precedence over everything else. I might be in the middle of a serious meeting with corporate executives or some investors when I would be unceremoniously interrupted by a sloppily dressed, boorish sounding trader who saw a large block of stock for sale at a compelling price. I could not restrain myself from some discussion of the opportunity, even if my elegant guests were temporarily put on hold. Equally, if my door was open to my colleagues, theirs was also open to me. I would often buzz the intercom box and have a trader or analyst come in, mostly when there was a problem. I am told they usually dreaded the call. "This stock is down three points," I would say, for example. "Why? What are we missing?" or "What do you know that the world does not know?" If the person did not have good answers, a discussion, sometimes heated, would ensue. I expected my analysts to know everything—indeed,

190

to know far more than I, who took ultimate responsibility for all of our investments.

I spent much of my time listening to investment ideas that covered the full spectrum of the marketplace—a range of industries about which, in many cases, I knew little. I became a very careful listener. For me to be effective in understanding these ideas and monitoring them over time, I constructed a system that overcame the necessity of specific knowledge across a wide range of industries. In short, I asked the right questions by seeking the variant perception inherent in each idea.

A summer intern reminded me years later of the advice I had given him on his first day at work. I told him that ideally he should be able to tell me, in two minutes, four things: (1) the idea; (2) the consensus view; (3) his variant perception; and (4) a trigger event. No mean feat. In those instances where there was no variant perception—that is, solid growth recommendations within consensus—I generally had no interest and would discourage investing. Moreover, I would purposely ask provocative, action-oriented questions. If an analyst bought a stock at 10 and it went up to 12, I would grill him or her: "Do you still want to own this stock? Are you willing to pay 12 for it?" If there was willingness to buy it at 12, then the stock should stay in the portfolio. If there was unwillingness to buy it at 12, then the stock might be sold.

The function of trading went beyond efficiently executing orders. It included being the eyes and ears of the portfolio. At times, through the flow of trading information, one might sense important fundamental change. There is great homogeneity in the community of research analysis, but sometimes the actual buyers and sellers tell a different story. We tried with our positions to learn what that story might be, particularly when trading activity was at variance with our expectation. Moreover, via active trading, often trading around a position, we achieved a feel for the market that could not be attained otherwise. We tried to coordinate our research and trading activities to take advantage of interim price movement. I liked to say that if we bought a stock at 20 having an objective of 30 through trading, we would hope to make profits equivalent to the stock going to 40.

I tried to view the portfolio fresh every day. Indeed, investing toward long-term capital gains treatment was of secondary consideration for me. Thus, there was an inevitable conflict between my constant measuring of the portfolio and the accumulated investment time that my analysts had in their positions and were loath to forgo. Stocks rarely go up or down in straight lines. Often, because of the intensity of my focus, I would sense that one of our positions was vulnerable in the short term and would be tempted to act. One of my favorite expressions was "the quick and the dead," meaning that if you did not respond fast enough to the newest change, even nuance, you might lose. The analyst, having spent tens of hours becoming intimate with the company, might resent my tampering with his or her position. I always felt that if an analyst could not strongly defend an investment, it should not be in our portfolio. I wanted my analysts to have strong convictions. Otherwise, their investments should not be held in the portfolio, particularly when there seemed to be short-term vulnerability.

I admit making many sales based on my shorter term perceptions, contradicting the views of my analysts, and sometimes being dead wrong. Thus, at times, my trading mentality infuriated some of my analysts. In late 1979, just after I had returned from my sabbatical, Oscar Schafer, an excellent analyst and a partner for many years, took a sizable position in Iowa Beef Processing (IBP). He knew the company well and bought the stock at an average cost of around $24 per share. We owned it for a month or two; during that time, it moved up to $29. One morning, I was antsy and anxious about the market. I called Oscar into my office and asked him, "Is this stock going up from here?"

He replied confidently that it was going up.

Not satisfied, I asked him, "When? What's going to get this stock moving? And when is that going to happen?"

He said, "I haven't got a clue where it's going short term. I only know I still like it long term and it's going higher."

Later that day, when Oscar came back from lunch, he punched up IBP on the Quotron in the trading room.

"Why are you checking that stock?" asked one of the traders. "Michael sold out your position while you were at lunch."

Four months later, an $80 tender offer was made for the company. I did not always make the right decision, especially when it came to trusting analysts.

Another time, Alexander Greenberg, an analyst who focused primarily on financial companies, was meeting with the management of the Bank of New York in their offices. During the meeting, Alex expressed our firm's enthusiasm for the financial sector in general and the stock of Bank of New York specifically. Fifteen minutes into the meeting, the bank's investor relations officer, who was seated facing a Quotron, remarked, "It seems your favorable long-term outlook for the financials has abruptly changed."

"What do you mean?" Alex asked.

"There was a headline that just came across on the Dow-Jones news tape announcing that Steinhardt Partners is believed to be the seller of several multimillion-share blocks of financial stocks that were liquidated in the market this morning. It seems that a block of 3.5 million shares of Bank of New York was included in the sales."

Needless to say, the meeting wound up shortly thereafter.

When Alex arrived back at the office, I explained to him that, while I deeply respected his analysis of these companies, my market view had changed and, when my view changed, I had no choice but to express it decisively. As I often said, "There are the quick and the dead."

Irregularly, my substantial turnover of the portfolio was itself exacerbated by my decision to "start all over again." I would decide I did not like the portfolio writ large. I did not think we were in sync with the market, and while there were various degrees of conviction on individual securities, I concluded we would be better off with a clean slate. I would call either Bob Mnuchin at Goldman Sachs or Stanley Shopkorn at Salomon Brothers and ask to have us taken out of the entire portfolio. In one swift trade, one of these firms would buy our longs and cover our shorts, often after extensive negotiation. In an instant, I would have a clean position sheet. Sometimes it felt refreshing to start over, all in cash, and to build a portfolio of names that represented our strongest convictions and cut us free from wishy-washy holdings.

⚬⚬⚬

The confrontational atmosphere I sometimes created in the office gave everyone an intensity and an edge that did not exist at most other firms. I thought, or at least persuaded myself, that this attitude drove every partner and employee toward excellence. I tried to lead by example. No one spent more time devoted to the business than I. Almost nothing occurred—no report, no statement, no opinion change, and no company announcement—without my being aware of it. Thus, everyone knew there was no avoiding the hard work necessary to be intellectually and informationally superior. Because I was highly self-critical, my expectations, while extreme, were mostly accepted.

Naturally, I was characterized as one of Wall Street's most difficult bosses. How could I justify my contentious behavior? How could I rationalize being outright unpleasant sometimes?

I kept going back to the fact that our investors were paying us "1 and 20" to perform for them. It was not my job to be nice, and I was never concerned about equanimity. It was not good enough to be a little better than the market because it was not our job to achieve a relatively good return. However much the market was down, we had to achieve an absolute, positive return. Our goal was to achieve the *best* performance, and we were always highly sensitive to and aware of what other good money managers were doing. I overtly stated that I wanted to have the very best performance of any money manager in America, and, for a fair number of years, I did just that.

This competitive intensity I shared with some of the best money managers in the business. In fact, if I were to judge any of the best money managers, including myself, simply on the quality of their long-term predictions, both macro and micro, the rating would be average at best. However, we would all score very highly on the competitive intensity scale.

I was tough and driven; sometimes, I said things that were too harsh and unfair. Each year was, in many ways, a war. I was the leader who led my troops past danger and on to victory. But it was tough going and sometimes there were casualties. I tried to get the best out of everyone, but did not always succeed. My burning intensity to perform motivated them to strive toward excellence. The people who truly understood that drive could cope with the stress. The one safety valve was that there was no carryover of feeling, at least, not on my part. Each day stood on its own.

⤳

This atmosphere became well known throughout the Street and led to some highly critical views of the firm. I was not immune to this sense that I was a tyrant with a bad temper who was at times unjustifiably dictatorial. However, I never lost self-confidence. I knew that my rigors, however difficult for those around me, were vital to the firm's success. Also, I knew no other way to operate. Following one of my "screaming tirades," I got back to business in short order. Some of the analysts, however, could not set the episode aside as readily as I could. They might shake, cry, or occasionally get physically sick from the experience. If I were ever measured as a builder of organizations, I would not get high grades.

Indeed, my managerial skill was so famously flawed that I once captured the interest of a fairly well-known psychiatrist—a distant friend who happened to be visiting my office one day. The shrink was fascinated with what he had heard and suggested that I could benefit from some "organizational therapy." He proposed spending a few months observing our firm and making some constructive suggestions to improve the dynamics. Being in a particularly good mood that day, I agreed to his proposal. What harm could come of it? Perhaps he could help me toward better control of my mood swings. Maybe I could get more out of my people if I improved my "organizational skills."

He began by meeting with each of my key employees and asking them to talk, confidentially, about what went on around the firm. They apparently used expressions like "battered children," "mental abuse," "random violence," "rage disorder," and so on. Several of them also warned him: "Just wait; Michael will get mad at you like he does everyone else, and will eventually throw you out of here." For a few months, the psychiatrist was everywhere. He would sit in my office and take copious notes. Sometimes he would listen to my conversations, including the heated discussions that often revolved around problem positions. He observed the harmony and disharmony of everything that went on, wrote detailed reports, and tried to analyze the dynamics of our office place. After a while, I began to find his presence to be a bit tedious.

Then one day, when I was particularly infuriated with an analyst over some investment that had clearly soured, I began my usual grilling. "How could you be so wrong? How could you keep giving me the same gibberish I've been hearing for the last four months while this stock has been killing us?" Then, when the answers continued to be unsatisfactory, as was the case most of the time, my face began to redden and I dramatically upped the volume, leaving my hapless confrere speechless. Our observing shrink stopped me. "Now Michael," he quietly said. "Calm down. Take a deep breath and think about this before you get yourself too worked up. Surely, there is a better way to deal with this." That was it. I had had enough. I told him to get the "@!%&$" out of the office before I threw him out the door. Perhaps my ying and my yang were inseparable and inevitably adaptive to the way I ran my firm. Whatever that means.

Needless to say, this intense, combative environment was not for everyone. In fact, over the years, many of my employees either did not make the grade or could not stand the pressure and created the impression that my firm had a revolving door. This legacy created a large contingent of Steinhardt alumni up and down the Street, many of whom started their own successful hedge funds. The joke was: "How much time did you do at Steinhardt?" Yet many ex-employees, generally the best of them, have also said that the time they spent working for me was the most formative of their investment careers. My alumni carried lessons that I taught them. They learned how to make money with me, and presumably that stayed with them long after the battle wounds had healed.

John Lattanzio was someone who managed to survive through multiple battles and many years of combat. He joined the firm soon after I returned from my sabbatical year, late in 1979. He was truly a self-made man. Never having graduated from high school, his use of the English language was consistent with his growing up in the Italian section of Astoria, Queens. He was an extraordinarily warm, likable, and generous person. His most remarkable quality was his lack of ego, which allowed him to develop intimate relationships with an extraordinary range of market professionals. Thus, John had a special rapport not only with senior traders and analysts at most major Wall Street firms, but also with a wide spectrum of money managers and highly acclaimed Ph.D. economists.

John played a number of vital roles as my head trader. Apart from the traditional execution of orders, and, because of his unique relationships, he was unusually aggressive in gathering ideas. The most important role John played, however, was in managing, better than anyone else, to lift my spirits when needed. He was also a buffer when I had gone too far verbally with other members of the team. His basic optimism created, in the firm, a feeling that usually offset my constantly ponderous nature. He had a terrific sense of humor. John had a range of routines that were funny even after they had been heard three or four times. His scatological repertoire was encyclopedic. His harangues toward women in the office were so filled with humor and good will that, coming from him, they were usually tolerated.

∞

Another unique characteristic of our firm was our casual dress. To say we were relaxed is an understatement. Nowadays, much of the business world, including the likes of Morgan Stanley and Goldman Sachs, think that the workplace, even the financial workplace, can dress casually. We were, from the start, light years ahead of the rest of the world in this respect. Because we were a firm with a reputation for being exceptionally intense, I persuaded myself that walking around in pullovers and Bermuda shorts would somehow ameliorate the pressure. This was not sartorial splendor. I would sometimes blanch when an important investor, perhaps a Swiss banker, would unexpectedly visit our offices and see our truly motley group.

Physically, our office always had a relaxed, unpretentious atmosphere, although others might use less complimentary terms. There were times in the 1990s when the trading room looked more like a war room. Every turret was occupied; we squeezed extra desks around the sides of the room. Boxes were piled everywhere. Phones were not only crowded on desks but strewn across the floor as well. Tapes were streaming, TVs were blaring, intercom boxes were everywhere, and, needless to say, people were shouting. Because we provided all employees with free lunches, partially eaten selections were on display well into the afternoon. When someone joined the firm as a new analyst, the guarantees were: a desk (perhaps in the hall), a phone, and, if one was ready, an individual line in the daily P&L runs.

After a while, Judy refused to visit the office because she could not stand the disarray. When we eventually moved from Thirty-ninth Street and Third Avenue to chic Madison Avenue, I was often asked if we intended to take along our old, torn, well-worn brown rug. Judy made sure that we did not.

In contrast to some other hedge funds' annual meetings for investors, which were elegant affairs, we were opposed to frivolous spending. In the early days, for our annual "gala," we rented folding chairs and provided our investors with sodas, peanuts, and potato chips. Normally, because they were very pleased with the content of the meetings and, particularly, with our performance, they never complained. I did, however, succumb on the twentieth anniversary of Steinhardt Partners to give a party at the Temple of Dendur at the Metropolitan Museum of Art. I even managed to enjoy myself.

❧

To offset the tensions in our frenetic environment, I tried to introduce some lighter moments. The humor tended to be slapstick and a bit immature, but it sometimes succeeded in relieving the pressure that would often build up during the day. One of my favorite amusements, particularly toward the end of a trading day, was to create fictional buy or sell orders. Some brokers who called did so for no reason other than to create a piece of business for themselves without any value added. When I sensed such a call, especially from a broker who was, in general, too aggressive, I would sometimes say to him, late in the trading day, "Go buy me 50,000 shares of Grumm. Use a 47 limit." Everything I said was perfectly audible except the symbol of the shares, which I had garbled. I quickly hung up the phone without giving the broker a chance to get the correct symbol. He would immediately call back, first to the trading desk (which knew nothing of my order, naturally, since there really was not one), then to my secretary. She would tell him I was in the bathroom. The trading day was nearing an end, with relatively few minutes left, and the broker had a seemingly large order he was not executing, no doubt creating extreme discomfort. With only moments to go in the trading day, he would call back, again frantic. This time I would pick up and quickly say, "It's late, if you have not completed the order at the 47 limit, buy it at the market." Again, I would hang up immediately. Naturally, the broker would call back in a panic, as the market was about to close. I would not take the call until the bell had rung, ending the trading day. Then, after the markets had closed, I would ask for my report.

At that point, he would nervously sputter, "I have a problem."

I would say, "No problem, just give me my report." Then I would hang up. Eventually, the entire trading desk would call him, laughing.

After a time, I played the prank too often and rarely got away with it. Fortunately, I had alternatives. For example, years after a company had been merged, or had folded, the name often remained in the minds of most brokers. Thus, I could successfully place an order to buy shares in Gimbel's, Montgomery Ward, Sinclair Oil, or a host of other no-longer-listed companies that seemed credible until the orders were taken to the floor of the New York Stock Exchange for execution and were met with harsh rebuke.

I had another favorite prank that sometimes worked well. Because of the active turnover of our portfolio, we were among the largest commission-paying accounts with the institutional block trading firms such as Goldman Sachs, Merrill Lynch, and Salomon Brothers. Occasionally, I would negotiate and complete a transaction with a senior trader while the salesperson who normally covered our account remained unaware of my involvement. It was the salesperson's job to call all clients whenever an important block trade took place.

The salesperson would call to announce a trade, saying perhaps: "We're trading 500,000 of Ford Motor at $24. Do you want to buy any?"

I would respond with: "Ford? I want to buy the whole block!"

The salesman would frantically shout across his firm's trading room, "I'll take everything!"

The trader would then shout back, "You bought 200,000 shares. Who are you?"

"I'm Steinhardt."

Then I'd hear the background noise, the shouting, the laughter, and inevitably, "You idiot! He's the seller!"

❦

For an investor who had a gross return of over 30 percent per year for 28 years, the number of "home runs"—shares where we had doubles or triples or more—in this period were surprisingly few. I always envied those who could buy a stock, ignore interim fluctuations, and, over a period, make a multiple on their investment. It seemed so elegant—divorced of most trading tensions and of course entitled to long-term gains at tax time. Alas, I mostly did not follow this approach. My gains were earned the hard way. I would kiddingly repeat, "Our investment style is 'four yards up the middle in a cloud of dust.'" I often wished it were otherwise.

I liked to think of myself as a fundamental value investor but, more often than not, I ended up selling too soon. I do not say that as a compliment à la Bernard Baruch, who said, "I got rich by selling too soon." My frenetic trading often resulted in leaving easy money on the table. A good example of this was our major involvement in International Business Machines (IBM), but the list is almost endless.

In mid-1993, we started buying IBM. Most analysts on Wall Street were negative. The consensus view was that IBM had lost its competitive edge. The stock had never really recovered from the 1987 crash and was totally out of favor with the Street. I love this kind of variant perception. While I was not technologically competent, I strained to understand the complexities of the computer business. I sensed that, with the massive write-offs IBM had taken again and again, and given its overall competitive strengths, whatever its problems, there would inevitably be a recovery. I just could not tell when. Louis Gerstner had just taken over as Chairman and Chief Executive Officer. I was one of the first investors to meet with him at company headquarters in Armonk, New York. Gerstner was genuinely pleased to learn that I was not only a supporter of his company but was among the largest shareholders.

The stock was depressed when we started buying, and we stayed the course, continuing to buy on weakness, even when IBM hit its absolute low. On some days, it felt like we were the only buyers out there. Then the stock turned and we continued buying as it started to move up. We had intended to acquire 20 million shares. However, we managed to buy only about seven million shares before the stock began to attract new buying momentum. Surrounded by the negativism, I cannot say I was totally immune. The Street was pessimistic and that, of course, is how bottoms are made in stocks and in markets.

We bought our seven million shares a little early. Six months later, we had made about 30 percent on our investment, which was fine but represented only a fraction of IBM's ultimate move. The problem was, as usual, we sold much too soon. By then, the consensus view had changed to positive. Money started flowing in, and the stock just kept going up, more or less in a straight line, for the next few years. Was I smart, or stupid, or just early?

Sometimes I think I sell early because I get far more pleasure out of taking on the intellectual challenge and being right than I do out of making the maximum return. Once I am proved right in the market, the bottom line is of less interest to me. I am ready for the next idea. As the underdog, IBM was exciting, and it felt good to go against the Street's misperception. By the time the stock turned around, I was ready to move on. The challenge was over. I have always been much more interested in picking a turn, an inflection point, than in playing an already existing trend. When everyone else decided IBM was a compelling investment, I was, unfortunately for me, long gone.

Warren Buffett has said, "If you are not willing to own a stock for 10 years, do not even think about owning it for 10 minutes." The truth of the matter is, I have never owned a stock for 10 years, but I have had the unique and profitable experience of owning some very good companies for 10 minutes.

∽

During the mid-1980s, we began relationships with some money managers outside of our firm—notably, those that offered a particular specialty that enhanced our skill set, like short sellers. One such group, the Feshbachs, three brothers from California, were, for a while, superb at finding what they called "terminal" shorts—companies that were frauds, bankruptcy candidates, or accounting fiascoes. They were often the target of vengeful companies whose Achilles heel they had exposed. The Feshbachs were able to successfully uncover a number of such companies—such as Cannon Group, L. A. Gear, and Cooper Companies—where we made close to 100 percent on our money. They also shorted numerous savings and loan companies, such as Landmark Land and Charles Keating's infamous Lincoln Savings and Loan, where we also did well.

But, the Feshbachs headed an unusual firm, to say the least. For one thing, they were all converts to Scientology, the religion founded by science fiction writer L. Ron Hubbard, which supposedly helped free people from psychological problems. It was never clear to me how Scientology played a role in their successful short selling. But, successful they were, for a good stretch of time, and with the bit of money that we farmed out to them, we did quite well. I should have had the foresight to see that their best days were behind them when, in 1991, they offered me a ride on their Challenger Jet. Rarely does a mix of overconfidence, science fiction, and new demonstrative wealth lead to continued success as a money manager.

One of our most frustrating shorts of all time was a small-ish purveyor of shopping and travel membership clubs: Comp-U-Card International, which eventually became CUC International. Our analyst, Herb Chen, had done an exceptionally good job in analyzing this company. He concluded that its earnings growth, which had been substantial, could not be maintained. Moreover, he was convinced that the company was engaging in highly aggressive and irregular accounting practices—simply put, it was "cooking the books." We began shorting the stock in 1989, and, like most positions, it was never supposed to develop into anything big—just another third-tier company with lousy accounting and a questionable business plan.

But, like many highly promotive companies, CUC's management was smart and persuasive and had a plausible, if convoluted, business plan. CUC presented a simplistic view of extraordinarily complex financial statements, and, in the process, corralled many of the most prominent institutional investors. Quarter after quarter, Herb predicted that the earnings would fall apart, and quarter after quarter he was wrong. I grilled him endlessly in my usual aggressive and unconstrained way. Yet, his answers were consistently solid and well grounded. He never "shot from the hip." He knew this company well, and as painful as the short was becoming, and as brutal as I was during our "sessions," I increased the size of the short, convinced that Herb would eventually be proven right.

Many stocks betray themselves by revealing the obviously speculative nature of their trading or ownership patterns. Not so with CUC. In contrast to other more speculative shorts, such as those involved with technological innovation or biotechnology where the volatility was at times frightening, being short CUC was a slow, steady grind. Against this backdrop, the firm wound up short millions of shares.

In 1992, CUC began a series of acquisitions designed to expand and reshape the company. Herb felt sure that these acquisitions were designed to mask the deteriorating fundamentals of the base business, but he also felt that management would probably be successful in its effort. After all, they had succeeded so far. Unlike many other shorts, which went out with a bang, this one went out with a whimper. I felt Herb was fundamentally right, but neither of us could stand another inexplicable quarterly earnings report. So we covered half the short and then covered half again. As the light at the end of the tunnel seemed to recede, we threw in the towel and covered our last share of this three-year short, eventually losing about $50 million on the position.

And there the matter rested—just another painful reminder of what happens when you sell what you do not own. Over the ensuing years, CUC continued its grinding advance, albeit without the noise associated with a large Steinhardt short position. In late 1997, however, the company merged with HFS Inc., another high-flying stock run by Henry Silverman. Within months, the new company, now renamed Cendant, owned up to massive accounting irregularities attributable to the old CUC divisions. The final postmortem provided by the SEC documented what Herb had suspected all along. Almost as far back as the company's inception, it simply made up numbers to suit its needs. Each year's fraud had to compensate for the previous year's fraud, so the manipulation grew larger each year. When the fraud got too big for one company, CUC bought other companies. When it got too big again, CUC merged the company into an even bigger company. By the end, it was the largest accounting fraud ever. It cost investors over $19 billion and involved the creation of over $500 million in fictitious profits. No solace to us.

# 13

# DABBLING IN POLITICS

**T**HIS FAMOUS KENNEDY QUOTE INSPIRED MANY of us growing up in the 1960s: "Ask not what your country can do for you. Ask what you can do for your country." Indeed, it helped form my sense of civic consciousness. Thus in the mid-1980s, when I consciously resolved to develop new interests beyond Wall Street, this notably included politics. I was attracted not by political candidacy but by the goal of generating and disseminating ideas that were important to me, and I thought could contribute to the political dialogue.

In the 1960s, surrounded by Brooklyn liberals, I supported Barry Goldwater. I abhorred the approach of left-leaning New York City politicians, including soon-to-be-elected Mayor John Lindsay, who were disingenuous in their civil rights advocacy. Moreover, these liberals were oblivious to the long-term financial and fiscal impact of their grandiosity. The liberalism that pervaded New York politics, as well as the National Democratic Party at that time, consisted of overripe precepts that would soon fall—or so I thought. The great political movement that had started in the 1930s with Roosevelt was now almost 30 years old and, despite a lack of new vigor, remained broadly popular. Thus I voted for Goldwater for president in 1964, almost in protest of the mass of left-wingers around me. The movement to the left in America soon peaked in the late 1960s, during the presidency of Richard Nixon, but my early conservatism was "ahead of the curve" and appropriate for the time.

Gradually, during the 1970s and the 1980s, I moved to the left as the world moved to the right. Whatever my ideology, however, I found the Democratic Party more sympathetic in terms of its constituencies, even though I remained far to the right of the Democratic mainstream. I continue to move to the left today, and the world continues to move to the right, but, I believe, not for too much longer. In the mid-1980s, while I was in the midst of this transformation, I got seriously involved in the recently created Democratic Leadership Council (DLC).

The DLC was founded largely to bring the party back to its historic mainstream. During the Reagan years, the Democratic Party had become so liberal it no longer appealed to most middle-of-the-road Americans. In the mid-1980s, the party was held together by minority and other special-interest groups. It was a party of blacks, Hispanics, unions, gays, feminists, and the elderly. Democrats were increasingly on the fringe, catering to specific factions. Republicans, meanwhile, had become the party of white middle-class Americans. In response to electoral losses in 1980 and 1984, the DLC was founded to counterbalance this splintering and bring the party back to the political center. At first, though, it cultivated only moderate–mostly Southern–Democrats such as Al Gore, Sam Nunn, and Chuck Robb. Those Southern Democrats attracted other Dixie Democrats, such as Senator John Breaux of Louisiana. I have a distinct memory of Senator Breaux leading a DLC convention in New Orleans by dancing as if he were leading a Mardi Gras parade. He is a keen politician who was destined to lead the DLC for a while, but I most envied him for his dancing.

My involvement with the DLC was based on a shared vision of the American future. For some (particularly, detractors) in the Democratic Party, the DLC was akin to Republicanism. That comparison really missed the point of the DLC, which was committed to a new vision for government: not liberal, not conservative, but progressive. In contrast, mainstream Republicans seemed narrow in their focus. Theirs was an almost unidimensional conservatism. The DLC, particularly its Board of Trustees, was composed of lay Democrats who were working with political theorists to create new ideas that would move the Democratic Party toward a progressive center. The phrases "moderate Democrat," "centrist Democrat," and "new Democrat" all evolved from the DLC. I soon became, by far, the DLC's largest financial contributor, donating a minimum of $250,000 per year for nearly 10 years. Early on, I became its legal chairman. We always had two chairmen, one for legal purposes and the other for political leadership. I also became chairman of the DLC's think tank, the Progressive Policy Institute.

More than anything else, I enjoyed the exploration and development of new ideas. I found that process as evocative as any intellectual pursuit. The concept of meshing one's idealism with contemporary political realities was very rewarding. Among these ideas were: National Service, fiscal discipline (a balanced budget), the earned income tax credit, charter schools, expanded trade (NAFTA, GATT, PNTR), welfare reform, urban development zones, and reinventing government. I was awed by the ease with which many of these ideas quickly became part of the national political dialogue. I felt a wonderful reaffirmation of the democratic processes, which had previously been only theoretical for me.

The Board of Trustees of the DLC held regular meetings in Washington, D.C., which I chaired. Members of this group were diverse in almost all respects except one; we were all relatively affluent. We came from all parts of the country, some conservative and some moderately liberal. We were of different ages and religions. Some of us had extensive political experience and others, like myself, none at all. Our mission was to mold ideas that had been formulated by DLC staff and ease their entry into the national dialogue. Often, there were elected officials present but their contributions were limited. The group had a freshness—there were disagreements but we all learned from the discourse. While dissimilar in many respects, we came together for the benefit of the party and the nation. There was a feeling of respect that led to pride in our innovation and a sense of being near the cutting edge. The creation of ideas by a group of citizens motivated by a national spirit took on a life of its own.

Early in 1989, Al From, president of the DLC, discussed with me the ongoing efforts to find a new political leader for our organization—a replacement for Senator Sam Nunn from Georgia, whose term as chairman was expiring. Al surprised me by mentioning a politician I had never heard of. He said, "I'm going down to Little Rock to meet with Governor Bill Clinton." The last notable thing Clinton had done, I soon learned, was give a speech at the 1988 Democratic National Convention that dragged on too long. As a result of this lengthy speech, he was in the political doghouse. Even worse, he had the reputation of being about as liberal as Southern Democrats can be. Al From said, "I want him to chair the DLC because Bill Clinton is the best political animal I've ever met. I'm going to tell him that if he's prepared to carry our message, we're prepared to make him a national figure." I thought for a moment about the incongruity of Clinton's left-wing liberalism and where we wanted to go. Nonetheless, I trusted Al's judgment and was prepared to back him.

Al went, Clinton accepted, and we were off on a new journey. That our views were perhaps inconsistent with his did not seem a serious encumbrance. Or maybe we were prepared to accept compromises from a leader with Clinton's charisma.

Clinton fell within the definition of moderate Democrat, but he was significantly apart from the DLC on issues of the day. He was a proponent of "big government" in his economic policies. His approach to upgrading Arkansas's inferior educational environment, his civil rights record, and his activities relating to the war in Vietnam created a distinct portrait. Historically, he was clearly a liberal and, to the degree we could judge, so was his wife. Not until Al From—a chubby little Jewish guy from Indiana, who lived and breathed political ideology—decided he was worth a makeover, did Bill Clinton begin to change.

∞

I met Bill Clinton for the first time in my apartment. I arranged for an evening with Clinton and Sam Nunn. They arrived together with Al From. I had also invited eight other couples who I thought could become interested in the DLC. Clinton wore very fancy cowboy boots. Nunn, prominent in national security and defense issues, was known to all my guests that evening, and he was to be the main attraction. But by the end of the evening, Clinton had captivated our group, particularly the ladies. As the pack of women swooned over Bill, Nunn stood in the background, virtually ignored.

Not too long after that first meeting, Clinton began calling me from time to time, late in the evening. After 11 o'clock, New York time, the phone would ring. I'd pick it up and an operator with one of those thick Arkansas accents would say, "Good evening, Mr. Steinhardt, sir. This is the governor's office, sir. Governor Clinton would like to speak with you, if you'd like to hold on, sir. One moment, for the governor." I would wait, and soon Clinton would get on the phone. "Hey, Michael, how ya doin'?" Sometimes his voice sounded lively; at other times, he sounded tired.

We would talk about contemporary issues impacting either the Democratic Party or the DLC. Jesse Jackson was one topic of conversation. At one point, From, Nunn, and Clinton had decided to exclude Jackson from speaking at the 1991 DLC convention. They reasoned that Jackson was the national symbol of liberalism, something the DLC was trying to move beyond. Nonetheless, the DLC had relatively few black constituents, so an unfortunate hint of racism would be associated with banning him. A conscious ban of Jackson would create political pressure on Clinton, and he was not comfortable with that possibility. Another Clinton phone call dealt with Middle Eastern policies. Basically, during these late-night conversations, we discussed whatever was on Clinton's mind, and that is how I came to know him.

∞

Clinton, following Al From's lead, incorporated the thrust of the DLC's message into his new national persona. He became the very embodiment of the "new" Democrat, the former liberal who had seen the light. Going into the 1992 election, we were all excited. After starting as an unknown long shot in the Democratic primaries, Clinton proved the wisdom of From's political judgment. We felt we were positioned right where America needed to be going. We also sensed that we had a better chance of winning the election than we had had in years. We were clearly right about moving the party toward the center, and, in articulating that message, Clinton was doing a better job than we had ever imagined possible. As the campaign progressed, I heard candidate Clinton pitch his own version of the DLC mantra with phenomenal resonance. Despite being the least known Democratic candidate, his charisma was refreshing and seemed to capture a great deal of public interest. He was frequently compared to JFK in appeal; his instincts seemed near perfect.

I was hopeful about the strides we were making as Clinton developed a national presence, but I soon discovered a side to the process that I did not like. Several people I knew on Wall Street aggressively solicited political contributions for Clinton because they had been given assurances that they would be awarded ambassadorships, or the equivalent, if they raised a certain amount of money—and if Clinton was elected. One in particular was perfectly comfortable announcing his fund-raising goal and its intrinsic tie to his personal future. As I found out more about how this game was played, and how good Clinton was at playing it, it started to sour me. I began to feel that many people who had joined the process, both elected politicians and professionals in the DLC, did not care one whit about ideas. Their goal was personal aggrandizement. Maybe I was simply naïve. Being a major fund-raiser or a supporter of elected officials held no allure for me.

Bill Clinton was elected in 1992, and those of us at the DLC thought that this was our great victory. Aside from his charm, the ideas that ultimately got him elected were a direct product of the work that had been done by the DLC since the mid-1980s. But, almost from the start, a separation developed between the new president and our organization. Few professionals at the DLC were appointed to the government positions they had sought. The differences in the policies adopted by President Clinton vis-à-vis those described by Candidate Clinton were palpable. The DLC seemed to have become part of his history, not his future. His early appointments and his early issues suggested that Clinton was not a "new" Democrat after all. Indeed, I came to believe that Clinton did not *have* a consistent philosophic center. For him, our work and our ideas toward creating a progressive approach to government were, at best, part of a repertoire that included a reversion to an older, left-leaning inclination.

Things didn't get any better, either. The first two years of the Clinton Administration were a disappointment. First, there was the gays-in-the-military issue, then the health care fiasco.

Next came some ultraliberal nominations and appointments in his cabinet and in the judiciary. It became obvious that Hillary, who was exercising considerable independence and authority, was to the left of Bill. I soon came to feel that my DLC involvement and the ideas created during that time were diminished by this new administration. Others in the organization felt the same way, and we started an ideological construct that we called "the third way." As an independent movement, "the third way" did not go very far. I remember having a meeting with then Senator Bill Bradley to inquire as to whether he might be interested in leading such a movement within the Democratic Party. When I proposed this to him, all six feet five inches of him stood up, walked from the far side of my office to a spot directly in front of me, and got down on his knees. He said, "I'm prepared to do many things in politics, but not commit political suicide. Running against a standing president of my own party would be just that."

My relationship with the DLC was becoming increasingly conflicted. It is often said that politics is the art of compromise, which I almost never had to do in my business life. Some trustees felt loyalty to the party. For me, ideas were primary. Some felt loyalty to President Clinton. I did not.

In the 1994 midterm election, Democrats sustained near staggering losses, largely because of disappointment with Clinton. In 1995, the DLC held its convention in Washington. I was traveling so I could not be there, but when I saw it on public television, with Bill Clinton as the guest of honor, I decided this was not the group I had hoped it would be, and I resigned at once. This was a precipitous act, a reflection of my naïve idealism, overemphasizing the purity of ideas over people and relationships in politics. Actually, ideas mattered little to most of the elected officials I came to know.

In retrospect, I acknowledge that I am not constitutionally cut out for the political world. Philosophically, I see things often

216

in black and white, whereas politics deals in grays. Politics is the art of persuasion, of compromise, and of coalition building. I dealt too much in absolutes that could be readily measured, like market performance, to function effectively in politics. Oddly, the effort we put into creating "the third way"—even that term— was openly absorbed by President Clinton and became an important concept during his second term. Indeed, he had the remarkable ability to learn from his mistakes early in his administration and to ultimately reconnect with DLC ideas and people.

There were other obstacles to my involvement in politics. My life in the stock market had made me accustomed to short-term results. At the end of each day, I could summon a profit-and-loss statement that told me all I needed to know. In politics, such a daily measure can only result in frustration. Policy shifts take years to formulate, and even longer to implement. Moreover, I am not sure how often there is clarity as to the actual success or failure of one's ideas. Al From would sometimes say that politics is a zero-sum game. People often say the same thing about financial markets.

Clinton's presidency will surely be the subject of continued debate, but, without a doubt, he is one of the great communicators in American history. In his presence, it is hard not to feel both respect and affection for him. Moreover, based on the economy, the stock market, growing globalization, and many other measures of well-being, the Clinton presidency was a success. However, as a role model—and I think this is most important—he has failed. In the end, his qualities as a role model will be remembered far longer than the economy he presided over.

Independent of the Clinton presidency, the DLC and the Progressive Policy Institute can be credited with many of the changes in American political dialogue in the last 10 years of the twentieth century. The Democratic Party has been fundamentally redefined from redistribution to growth, from welfare to work, from soft on crime to tough, and from big government to a "re-invented" smaller bureaucracy. These ideas have become the model for the resurgence of center-left politics all over the world. And I believe this will endure.

∞

I remember one story all too well about Bill Clinton. One night, during the 1992 campaign, I was having dinner with Al From at a New York restaurant, An American Place. Everything in the campaign was going well. Clinton had come from nowhere to be the Democratic nominee. Al was now recognized as a political strategist of note.

We had not yet begun dinner when his assistant left to take a phone call. When she returned to the table, I could see her face was flushed. She whispered something to Al, and he looked a little discomforted. I looked at them both and said, "What's going on?"

Al acknowledged to the assistant that she could tell me. "I just heard," she said, "that tomorrow there's going to be an article in the *Star* about a woman named Gennifer Flowers. She is going to say that she had a twelve-year affair with Bill Clinton. He is going to deny this."

I absorbed the information. Then I looked at Al and said, "Do you think it's true?"

He looked back, smiled, and said, "Michael, Bill has always been a man of great appetites." Time would tell.

# 14

# THE WORST YEAR
# OF MY LIFE

**D**URING THE EARLY 1990S, OUR CAPITAL BASE grew enormously. Everything that we invested in worked spectacularly. Our performance was superb, three consecutive 60 percent years, and with that came a newfound recognition. The bull market of the past decade had made many people rich and had created new interest in aggressive money management. It seemed that every "sophisticated" investor wanted to participate in hedge funds, perhaps because their cachet denoted a peculiar exclusivity. Hedge funds became a buzz word. Our firm was bombarded by potential investors who were begging us to let them invest. I could not attend a social event without being besieged with requests to take money from potential investors. This made it easy to develop hubris and, unfortunately, I was not immune.

Unless constrained, a hedge fund with excellent performance over time will grow rapidly, double charged with both internal returns on capital and enhanced reputation. In 1993, we launched our fourth fund, Steinhardt Overseas Fund, Ltd., our second offshore fund. We were now running just under $5 billion, an enormous amount back then, and even now. As our asset base grew—both because of our performance and because we opened our funds to new investors, albeit on a limited basis—we began to reach for larger, now global, markets to employ the capital, even as we continued to run a huge portfolio of domestic stocks. More and more, we moved into the "macro" arena, a term used to describe investing in global stock, bond, and currency markets. Having been successful in the markets that I had ventured into over time, I had confidence that the quality of my investment judgment was applicable worldwide. Perhaps rapid success had bred complacency.

Furthermore, it had become harder for our traditional positions in domestic equities, particularly those in small or mid-capitalization companies, to have a meaningful impact on the portfolio. The challenge became finding investment opportunities that were large enough to employ our expanded capital base in a way that could contribute to the overall performance of the capital under management. We wanted not only to be right in our views but also to have enough money invested in each idea to justify the time committed to researching it. It took no more time to be intellectually competitive in a $20 million investment than in a $2 million investment.

With growing confidence, and with swelling assets under management, we began to hire people with a more global range of investment experience. We added international portfolio managers and analysts, economic consultants, and "think tanks" to our payroll. It became vital to expand our intellectual resources commensurately with our financial resources. Overnight, it seemed, we needed a team that could competitively analyze and invest in markets around the globe.

Invariably, in its early stages, this type of expansion is filled with risk. I, who had never been a model manager of personnel, now found myself spearheading an organization of more than 100 people who were trading across a spectrum of financial markets around the globe. With more assets in more places, my role of understanding each and every position became exponentially harder.

I used to say, not quite kiddingly, that I would never invest in a country where I did not know the area code. Now I found myself tempted to own fledgling companies in the hinterlands of Brazil, Venezuela, Morocco, Zimbabwe, and even the former Soviet Union, where recently converted ex-communists were now virgin capitalists. Suddenly, with my new team and newfound global perspective, I was actively trading the French CAC 40, the German DAX, and the Japanese Nikkei indexes. Through derivatives, we shorted volatility in the United States, Japanese, and German equity markets. Along with international equity markets, fixed-income opportunities, remote and familiar, were now available to us. Unfortunately we walked forward unafraid.

In Europe, monetary union was hotly debated. This uncertainty created speculative opportunities in French bonds (OATs and BTANs) and futures (notionals), German bonds (BUNDs and OBLs), Italian bonds (BTPs), and Spanish bonds (BONOs). We put on convergence trades between the government debt of Canada and the United States, the United Kingdom and Germany, Italy, and Spain. We initiated swap spreads (fixed vs. floating rates) in France, Italy, and Japan. We held directional bets on the debt of most of Europe, Australia, New Zealand, Japan (JGBs), and other countries. Boldly venturing into foreign exchange markets, we held multiple currency cross-trades, including Mark/Swiss, Sterling/Yen, and Mark/Paris. We had a sizable bet on the continued strength of the dollar across the board. My daily Profit and Loss (P&L) Statement was now 30 pages long and read like the German code from World War II. To further complicate matters, our methodology for calculating risk, while accurate, was tedious and behind the times. I found myself trying to be at least knowledgeable about names that, six months earlier, I had never heard of.

Many of the new opportunities in international markets allowed the firm to employ significantly greater amounts of leverage. Moreover, Wall Street was flush with bull market success, and credit, at attractive terms, was readily available. New derivative products (bets that hinged on the price of underlying securities) abounded, required almost no money down, and created unseen leverage in the portfolio.

We purchased and then repurchased (financed) our enormous bond portfolio for as little as a 1 percent "haircut" (collateral). This meant that for every $100 million of bonds, we sometimes had to utilize only $1 million of capital. By 1993, we were more confident than ever, and our foreign bond portfolio totaled more than $30 billion. With each basis point (a one hundredth of a percentage point) move in bond yields, we made or lost $10 million. We had come a long way from King Resources or even from our first bond triumph in the early 1980s.

In particular, 1993 had been a fabulous year. We were up more than 60 percent, primarily because of our significantly levered bet on European bonds—mostly, German bunds and French betans. Then, in the fourth quarter, U.S. economic growth surged, prompting the Federal Reserve to begin raising short-term interest rates for the first time in five years. On February 4, 1994, the first rate hike of one quarter of a percentage point caught us and many other leveraged bond players off guard. We were wrong in thinking that our optimistic interest rate outlook would continue. Because we were heavily leveraged, the consequences were grave.

United States bonds toppled, but the losses in domestic treasuries paled in comparison to the hits taken in European markets, which were much less liquid. In Europe, the selling was also sparked by fears that the Bundesbank would halt the trend under way to ease credit. The rise in U.S. interest rates made U.S. bonds relatively more attractive than other global fixed-income opportunities and, with a jolt, these markets fell precipitously. Catching me unaware, European bonds plummeted as liquidity dried up. In addition, we held small positions in some emerging bond markets, and these too fell apart.

In periods such as this, exits quickly become small and crowded. We soon discovered that far too many other "speculative" investors like ourselves (i.e., other hedge funds) had made the same bets in European bonds. Their lack of experience, like ours, compounded the absence of liquidity. Emboldened by their success in investing abroad during a sustained period of declining interest rates, much of the hedge fund world had ventured into newer, broader, less efficient markets as well. In short, the trade in European bonds was crowded, a fact that totally passed me by.

To make matters worse, the proprietary trading desks of the major brokerage firms—including Bankers Trust, Merrill Lynch, J. P. Morgan, and Goldman Sachs—had made some of the same bets on foreign bonds. There was a substantial overlap between our positions and theirs. Ordinarily, one's broker or dealer is there to make markets and provide reasonable liquidity, even in times of need. But the trading desks themselves were overextended in their positions, and they too were competing with us to make sales. Furthermore, Askin Capital Management, a hedge fund that specialized in trading leveraged mortgage securities, collapsed during this period, forcing the trading desks at some of the big firms to further curtail their market making. Suddenly, events that were not ordinarily connected were.

One point cannot be overemphasized: Global bond markets were, for me and for too many other leveraged hedge funds, a relatively new medium. I was experienced in dealing with liquidity, constraints, and leverage in many markets, including the U.S. bond market, but the European markets were new ground. With our new and relatively inexperienced team, we simply were not on top of the game. Without knowing it, our confidence had lured us into becoming too big in these markets. The instincts that had been honed in me during the decades of dealing with domestic stocks were simply not applicable. I had prided myself in having an edge in most investments. Instead, I was caught investing in countries where I did not profess to know, or even want to know, the area code.

In these markets, there simply was not the same flow of information. Moreover, it was not exactly clear where I stood on the chain of knowledge. When it came to forecasting geopolitical and economic trends, I did not have a competitive or intellectual advantage. The normal flows of input, which would usually ring warning bells in the domestic financial world, were perhaps somewhere on a distant continent. There I was, reliant on new people with whom I had never before been in the trenches. It was a formula for disaster.

I had misjudged the liquidity of the positions we held. Now, faced with a massive sell-off, there was no painless way to get out. Traders know that, in times of market stress, they sometimes need to sell what they can sell, regardless of price. The sad irony was that everybody else needed liquidity at precisely the same time that we did, so there was not much selling to be done.

We watched the screens in awe as wave after wave of sellers threw in the towel. Everyone was looking for a bid but there were no bids to hit. In my February monthly letter to investors, I reported that we were already down almost 20 percent and we were not out of many positions yet. My traders were shell shocked and hoped that the worst had been seen, but because we, and most others who had crowded into the same trade, had not yet sold much, they were wrong. After the market started its decline, we sold some bonds; as it went down more, we sold more; and so on. Even worse, it seemed that every time we went to sell, the Street knew what we were doing and followed.

John Maynard Keynes said: "Markets can remain irrational longer than you can remain solvent." Thus it is rare, particularly with leveraged securities, that one can endure a substantial decline without being a victim of it. Even if one has great confidence in a position, which then declines substantially, the process by which the loss is experienced is always so unnerving and detrimental that the position is a victim of the decline itself. Price creates its own reality. Obviously, dramatic declines often end with liquidations at the bottom. This is the insidious impact of panic and leverage. We felt it.

But I would be wrong to characterize myself as simply a victim of a liquidity squeeze or an unexpected market turn. If I was a victim of anything, it was of hubris or unjustified confidence in my own abilities—perhaps the result of too many too-easy successes. In the end, I was responsible for thinking that I could successfully conquer a spectrum of markets around the globe. I had lost sight of my own limitations. I was shocked and humbled by my failure.

I was also wrong to think that because I held positions in various global markets, my portfolio was truly diversified. If so, it might then have provided some reduction in the overall risk. In times of stress, inevitably, markets that are not normally correlated suddenly are. I might have learned this lesson during the 1987 debacle, but I now ignored it. There was no one at the firm whose judgment I could rely on. Again, I felt alone.

We finally finished liquidating the entire portfolio at the end of March, only three months into the year. At that point, we were down 30 percent. I felt more depressed than I had ever been. This was worse than 1987. That crash had only negated most of our work for the year; we actually posted a slight gain. Now, we were down, way down. Indeed, this was by far the only substantial loss the funds had ever suffered. Our only other loss years had been 1969 and 1972, when we were down by approximately 1.5 percent in each year. I had failed in the most fundamental tenet of money management: capital preservation.

The *Wall Street Journal*'s blaring headline declared that I had lost a billion dollars. Reporters besieged me with questions, wanting to know what it felt like to lose so much money. I was too numb to be able to identify my emotions. I dreaded each new inquisitive call. Answering reporters' questions was unmitigated pain, not to mention a huge distraction. Moreover, my investors, who were extraordinarily supportive throughout the years, and with whom I had developed many close friendships, now intensified their efforts to be encouraging, despite the setback. Inadvertently, they added to my discomfort. With few exceptions throughout my career, my investors had been exemplary. I could not have asked for a more loyal group, and their spirit and support normally inspired me. But during this period, the only real solace I could receive came from my family. Judy and our kids did their best to persuade me that this was not the end of the world. David, in particular, himself new to the investment business, nevertheless had some understanding of what was going on. His support stood out in an otherwise bleak landscape but even that was not enough.

⋘⋙

In the midst of this debacle and my subsequent depression, I received visitors in my apartment late one night. We had just come home from celebrating David's 25th birthday. My team of lawyers, having returned that day from the Securities and Exchange Commission (SEC) in Washington, had some unpleasant news. A government inquiry that had begun in 1991 had suddenly taken a turn for the worse. The firm was about to be formally accused of colluding to corner the market in two-year U.S. Treasury notes.

The theory put forth by the SEC, the Justice Department, and other government agencies was that Salomon Brothers, Steinhardt Partners, and Caxton Corporation, run by Bruce Kovner, had bought up prohibitive amounts of two-year Treasury notes in April and May of 1991. Specifically, they accused us of colluding to acquire enough of the bonds, and thereafter to finance in such a way as to control the market. We denied we had done anything wrong in taking our large Treasury note position.

Our substantial investment in Treasuries had begun much earlier, in mid-1990, and was motivated by my conviction that interest rates would fall. It had been nine years since my last serious foray into the bond market, but I began to sense the opportunity was again ripe. The economy was vulnerable, and the federal government would have little alternative other than to reduce short-term interest rates. Our expectations proved correct in 1990, and our funds did quite well. Then, in early 1991, with the successful conclusion of Operation Desert Storm ("We're No. 1!"), there were consensus predictions of a vigorous emergence from the recession. We believed those predictions to be optimistic. As the market rose, we increased our short positions in equities, and as bond prices declined, we increased our long positions in Treasury notes. Beginning in March, yield curve changes led us to concentrate heavily in two-year notes. I calculated time and time again, using various interest-rate scenarios for a range of time frames, where on the yield curve a leveraged bet, sometimes called a "carry trade," would achieve the best return with the least amount of risk. That judgment proved correct not only with regard to the broader economic environment but also with respect to the two-year notes offering the best opportunity on the curve. We continued to buy Treasuries and aggressively participated in the April and May two-year auctions.

Then, in June 1991, the government began investigating price fixing or collusion at auctions. It was alleged that Salomon and three key clients—Tiger Management (run by Julian Robertson), Quantum Fund (run by George Soros), and the Steinhardt funds—had colluded to manipulate the market in two-year Treasury notes issued in the April and May auctions. In August 1991, the federal probe widened amidst revelations by Salomon that it had submitted falsified bids in Treasury auctions on behalf of customers. Tiger and Quantum were dropped from the investigation, but the probe against us continued and now included Caxton Corporation.

In time, the SEC issued subpoenas to key people at Salomon, Caxton, and Steinhardt. An uproar developed, largely related to Salomon Brothers, that forced its leading executives to resign and resulted in Congressional hearings. There, Warren Buffett, who had taken over as the new chairman of Salomon, revealed that his firm, along with customers (including us), had in fact owned as much as 94 percent of those notes. While "cornering a market" is, in fact, legal under most circumstances, it was alleged that we had conspired together to trigger the squeeze.

Eventually, a large group of small investors filed a number of class-action civil suits, later rolled into one suit, against Salomon, Caxton, and Steinhardt. They alleged that these markets were a zero-sum game, and that we had colluded to squeeze the notes, which they were short, causing them to lose millions.

The unfolding investigation dragged on for two years, 1992 and 1993. Meeting after meeting took place. Every scrap of paper and every conversation and detail relating to the notes were turned over to the government by our lawyers. It took endless time. Finally, in March 1994, at the very same time the

European bond market was crashing and I was facing the greatest financial loss in my career, the three firms involved in the Treasury investigation agreed to forge a settlement. We all went along with the settlement without admission of guilt. I released a statement, published in the *Wall Street Journal* on March 31, 1994. "We're participating in the settlement," I said, "in order to reduce the continued burden, expense, and distraction of protracted litigation. The firm continues to deny it engaged in any wrongdoing."

We ended up paying the SEC and Justice Department civil fines to alleviate the burden of these ongoing investigations. All in all, we at Steinhardt paid fines and fees totaling more than $70 million. While denying wrongdoing throughout, we had reached the point where we needed to move on. The continued distraction of protracted litigation had taken its toll.

Next, we began discussions at Steinhardt Partners about how we were going to divide up the payment of fines and legal fees among the partners. In the end, we decided to pay all fines and legal expenses out of the General Partner's allocation from the funds; thus, I paid 75 percent of the fines. Our investors never paid a penny of the fines, nor of the legal expenses.

Despite the enormous burden of the Treasury scandal, our bond bet had been a huge win for our investors. From mid-1990 through 1993, we had made more than $600 million on our interest-rate view. The strength of our conviction about the economy, interest rates, and the yield curve had motivated our aggressiveness in having a large leveraged Treasury note position, in many ways analogous to 1981 and 1982. We had a well-founded, publicly articulated view of interest rates and the economy, and we had the courage to make an enormous bet on being right. It had paid off handsomely for our investors even though, because of the scandal, it left me wounded.

The scandal and its aftermath brought out problems I had not anticipated. One General Partner, Charles Davidson, left as a result of the Treasury inquiry against the firm and the subsequent settlement. Chuck had done well for us. An expert in distressed securities, he had been responsible for a number of successful investments, including our profitable adventure in Sunbeam Corporation. For his investment skills, I respected Chuck.

Along with my reputation for being a demanding boss, I also had a reputation for compensating my employees generously. In the years leading up to 1994–specifically, 1991, 1992, and 1993–the firm made an enormous amount of money, much of it from positions we took in bonds. For those three years we were up close to 60 percent per year. Because so much of our profits had come from our Treasury notes position, I was disturbed when some partners refused to stand by me in this tough time. This was shaping up to be the worst year of my business life.

I remember being so badly dispirited on Good Friday that I could hardly function. Judy told me I looked terrible. My friends told me I was in bad shape. My partners had never seen me like this. The culmination of events had taken its toll, I took everything personally and everything was going wrong.

Beginning in February, we had experienced substantial foreign bond losses. In March came the tremendous burden of the Treasury scandal. Next, the squabbles between my partners took a further toll. By summer, having had no success in turning around the portfolio, I was at my wits' end. I was mad at myself, mad at the government for harassing us over a case I believed had no merit, and mad at the partners who were leaving me. I dreaded coming into the office in the morning, but I had no choice. I began to fantasize about leaving the business. But I had an added problem. Given the kind of career I had had, there was no way I would leave my investors at the end of a bad year.

The final numbers proved it. At year's end, we were down 31 percent. It was the one year in which I actually lost a meaningful amount of money. In 1987, I had given back the profits we had made earlier in the year, but I did not lose money. In this year, I truly lost a great deal of money, and, even with all the years of success, this failure dominated my life. I could focus on nothing else. However, the only redeeming part about ending an awful year is that you wipe the slate clean and start all over again.

I had to try and put everything into perspective. After all, from July 1967, when we first opened Steinhardt, Fine, Berkowitz & Company, until the end of 1993, the funds' annual returns had averaged 33.5 percent. Even so, I anguished over 1994 as if my entire career had been a failure. I could not avoid feeling as if my very worth as a human being depended on my continually making money. What was I worth when I lost?

# 15

# "STEINHARDT QUITS!"

I SOMETIMES SAID WORKING AT STEINHARDT Partners was like playing major league baseball and I was the player-manager. From the first day of employment, I would immediately give someone the opportunity to come to bat. I would encourage the player to stand in the batter's box and swing at almost any pitch that he or she was tempted by. Quicker than most, I could tell whether the player was going to be able to make it on my team. Other firms would offer a six-month or one-year trial time; this was not the case with me. Players immediately became part of the action. I looked for the quality of intellect as it was reflected in the way the newcomers played the game and the way they articulated their game plan. If they could not make it, that was not a broad condemnation. It just meant they could not play for me. My reputation for toughness and high standards left little blemish on anyone who came and then went. When it was time for someone to move on, I would always do everything to make sure a good job was landed.

For me, the bottom line was all that mattered. I needed to give my clients spectacular performance. To do that, I sought to have the absolute best in the business working for me. The goals I set for myself were often unrealistic. Many people had a hard time living up to my prohibitively high standards. For this I did not apologize.

By the same token, I recognized that, as any major league baseball player knows, there inevitably comes a time when even the best in the game have to retire. Everybody tops out sometime. Even though I was only 54 years old, I now felt, more strongly than ever, that it was time for me to quit the business. I had certainly had my run. By this point in my career, I had made my mark on Wall Street. Investing other people's money no longer offered the psychic rewards that it once did. I had accomplished everything I had dreamed of, and made more money than I had ever imagined. I had achieved an outstanding record. More and more, I came to feel that the highs from success were not quite as high as in the past, and the lows seemed much lower. Certainly, 1994 was the lowest of the lows. 1987 was bad enough, but at least I had bounced back and had a string of six outstanding years. Then in 1994, we had lost, and we lost big. 1987 had shaken me; 1994 had been devastating. It had taken a part of me that could not be retrieved.

As 1995 began, I was resolved to recoup the losses of the previous year. Yet, I did not have a totally clear vision. I was apprehensive. Moreover, for many years, I had been frustrated by my inability to build a quality organization that could be independent of my leadership. Now I felt particular despair. There was no one to "turn over the reins" to, no successor. In too many ways, I had run a one-man show, and I was tired of performing. I had hired plenty of competent people over the years, but I could never successfully delegate investment decisions in their entirety. At times in the past, I had mused about leaving the firm to my associates, my general partners, but I did not have the confidence to entrust my investors' money to them. The Steinhardt organization's administrative side, run by Herb

Newman until his death and later by Lisa Addeo, ran smoothly, year after year, with almost no turnover. Yet, finding, developing, and keeping the best investment staff was a perennial problem. I put the blame on my own unrealistic expectations.

By the spring, I had shared my apprehension with several key partners, and we began to discuss the possibility of closing the firm. I would not consider selling it; I could not envision a firm with my name on it being run by someone else. At one point, years earlier, I had received an offer from Dreyfus Corporation to buy a minority interest in the firm. I turned it down. Much later, we worked with Merrill Lynch toward the creation of what would have been one of the largest and most lucrative closed-end funds ever. Close to the launching point, I changed my mind. I could not accept the idea of seeing my name, Steinhardt, in the financial pages when it represented an entity that I did not steer. Throughout my career, I had taken responsibility for my firm's results. When investors put their money with me, they knew they were buying a piece of me— my instincts, my experience, my intensity, my soul. Thus, I could not conceive of someone trading under the name Steinhardt without me, unless it was my son, David.

As the year progressed, I considered how I was enjoying my days. I easily envisioned future years of superior performance and oversized compensation, to assess how rewarding this continued prospect might be. On a day-to-day basis, making money in the investment business, with all its intensity, is mostly fun—not necessarily profound or deep, but fun. The alternative I was now seriously contemplating—leaving the business—seemed like walking into an abyss I had flirted with previously. I had certain ideas about what I wanted to accomplish if and when I left the business, but what did they mean relative to the decades-old routines to which I had grown so accustomed? I could not make up my mind.

Day to day, I waffled. If I closed the door, returning several billion dollars in assets, I was walking away from a firm I had spent 28 years building. When one devotes most of one's life to building almost any type of business, it is usually either sold or passed on to others upon one's retirement. Here, I would be closing the door, giving up the values created and the streams of income. I would be leaving and taking my name with me. I had taken a sabbatical year, so this would be my second departure from the business. But if I quit this time, I would not come back. "Are you going to pull the trigger, Mike?" my chief trader, John Lattanzio, would ask me. I simply could not give him an answer. The truth was, I did not know. I changed my mind weekly. I continued to hold meetings with lawyers and key staff members, to try and reach a decision. At this point, one of my main concerns was to recover from 1994. I had to make money back for my investors. I would not go out after the only bad year of my career. We had to make it back. We did, too.

In June, *Forbes* characterized me as a "chastened bear" or, perhaps more accurately, as a "reluctant bull." A substantial portion of our equity portfolio was invested in blue-chip financials such as Sallie Mae, Federal National Mortgage, Bank America, and First Union Bank. My single biggest investment was Chemical Bank; I owned 2.7 million shares at the time the bank announced plans to merge with Chase Manhattan. I was also very positive on insurance companies; the industry was ripe for the kind of consolidation that was sweeping banking. Thus, we had large holdings in many insurance stocks, including Aetna and Travelers. It began to look as if the portfolio was well positioned and we were going to have a good year.

While I was making my final decision, I kept the possibility of my retiring under wraps. There was no indication publicly that I might be leaving the business, although I had often discussed it with close friends. The time constraint associated with the possibility of retiring put an additional stress on the investment process. Clearly, I had to be sensitive to liquidity so that I could convert the portfolio to cash if necessary. It was like a football game with only a few minutes to go.

By September, our funds were up about 22 percent. (We would eventually end the year up 26 percent.) The performance was sufficiently good to create the window I was looking for. I made up my mind. We had recouped most of the 1994 loss. My investors were happy. I could feel good about returning their money. I decided to pull the trigger.

Many people in the firm had heard me speculate about quitting so often that I had become "the boy who cried wolf." This did not disturb me; I always had a willingness to talk openly about issues, even those that required considerable sensitivity. I knew, as difficult as it was, that I had to stay beyond the terrible 1994 and get back to my winning ways. Now, however, I had crossed the Rubicon, and my decisions were internally motivated. What others said did not matter.

All of us at Steinhardt had made a lot of money over the years. I had made my investors more money than they could have earned investing with perhaps any other money manager. Year after year, I posted some of the highest returns on Wall Street. Proud of what I had achieved, I was thrilled to have had a career that was being called "legendary." But it was time to move on.

I could say I had been among the very best in the business. Now I wanted to start again, doing something noncommercial that might give me a different and more meaningful fulfillment. I decided to do something I had been thinking about for a long time. I would try to create and pass along some kind of legacy that would supersede making money. I would devote myself to the cause that resonated most, the future of the Jewish people.

In early October, I told my general partners that I planned to announce to the firm, the Street, and the public that I was retiring and closing down all the Steinhardt funds.

∞

On the morning of October 11, I called my entire firm together: partners, traders, analysts, portfolio managers, back office staff, everyone. We gathered in our large conference room. Judy joined us.

Just before making the announcement, I had my partners call our brokers and alert them to what was about to happen. It was important for them to know that no portfolio problems were driving the plan. Perhaps 12 of our top brokers got the confidential heads-up call from my office, explaining that I was closing the firm. Simultaneously with my announcement in the conference room, we issued a press release over the financial wire.

As I stood at the podium and looked out at the roomful of my people, many of whom had worked for me for years and were still hopeful that, even at this last moment, I would change my mind, I started to speak. I had not prepared a script. I just talked.

"This was a very hard decision for me," I said. "I love this business as much as anything, and I find it hard to separate myself from it. But after thinking about this for a very long time, I've made the difficult decision to close the firm at the end of December."

Because I had pondered doing this before but had not done it, many people in the room did not believe I was actually going through with it. As I spoke, some of them started to cry. It was a very emotional moment for me, as it was for them, but in spite of my feelings, I maintained my composure.

"This business has been my life," I went on, "but it's now time for me to move on to the next phase. I will miss you all. I will miss this business. But everything must come to an end."

❧

I was quite surprised and flattered by the media attention my announcement received. The financial press and the New York dailies covered the story of my retirement. One New York paper summed it up in a succinct headline: "Steinhardt Quits!" Its lead sentence read: "Michael Steinhardt yesterday sensationally quit Wall Street, marking the apparent end of one of the most meteoric careers in the world of finance." Various articles detailed the history of my performance. One of the most common statistics quoted pleased me: One dollar invested with me in 1967 would have been worth $481 on the day I closed the firm in 1995, versus $19 if it had been invested in a Standard and Poor's index fund. One of my early investors, Richard Cooper, a Chicago businessman, told *Time* magazine he had invested $500,000 with me 28 years ago, and, at the time of our closing, that amount had grown to over $100 million.

On October 15, the *Washington Post* ran a retrospective article on my career. The piece included a long quote from me on the issue of investing: "The hardest thing over the years has been having the courage to go against the dominant wisdom of the time, to have a view that is at variance with the present consensus and bet that view. The hard part is that an investor must measure himself not by his own perceptions of his performance but by the objective measure of the market. The market has its own reality. In an immediate, emotional sense, the market is always right. So if you take a variant point of view, you will always be bombarded for some period of time by the conventional wisdom as expressed by the market."

I was also asked by the *Post* to give my market views and worldviews. "I think we are in the midst of a great bull

243

market, an extraordinary bull market," I said. "Never in our lifetime has a smaller percentage of the world's resources been spent on the military. Never in our lifetime have people lived so much longer in so many parts of the world. You can count the number of rogue dictatorships on one hand: Iraq, Iran, Libya, Cuba, and North Korea. The world in the broadest sense has become a much, much better place. We are experiencing the great benefits of the political swing to the right that has occurred in the United States and the world, where the battle for the minds of men has been won by a benign capitalism. Consumerism is the only ism that seems to count anymore, not fascism, not communism. Labor has become just another element, another cost in the production process, as you would view sand, or tin, or steel. That has made for higher profits and a greater acceptability of capitalist values. That is what you need to understand the bull market."

Since 1995, we have continued to experience an extraordinary bull market, and stock prices have risen to breathtaking levels that were barely conceivable when I closed the business. Although we are currently in the first bear period in many, many years, I believe that the world continues to be a much better place than at any time in history.

☙

So, we closed the firm. We had come up with severance packages for the administrative personnel. As before, I was generous with employees. We needed some staff to remain through year-end; by that time, almost everyone had another job. My employees were, in fact, besieged with job offers.

Besides dealing with internal issues, we had to finish liquidating the entire portfolio so that we could return most monies by the end of the year (or close to it) when the Steinhardt funds officially ceased activity. The liquidation process ran smoothly. Between October and December, we gave investors back 85 percent of their money. By January 10, 1996, we had brought the total up to 90 percent. As of April 1996, we were up to 95 percent or more. A few illiquid positions, which could not be initially sold or that had liabilities attached, were set up in special accounts. In the liquidation process, I was determined to get the absolute top dollar for every position. I agonized over the sale of our assets, as I did over every trade I had made in my career. I wanted my investors to get the best possible price they could for every investment. I would not compromise. That was the way I had run Steinhardt Partners, and that was the way I was going to run my firm until its last day.

∞

After we closed down, Judy and I took a two-week vacation. Upon my return, I had to deal with the reality that I had, in fact, retired. In retirement, I would keep my office but with a much smaller staff. I had no traders working for me, but on the first day back, creature of habit that I was, I did what I always did. I sat at my desk, looked at my Bloomberg screen flashing stock quotes, and decided I wanted to trade. The problem was, I did not have a trader to place orders with the brokerage firms. I picked up our years-long direct line into the Goldman Sachs trading room. "Hi, this is Mike Steinhardt," I said to the broker who answered. "I want to buy a few S&P futures." Then I dictated the orders to him. It was just like the old days, when I entered orders myself without going through the trading desk. I listened carefully as he read them back to me before I hung up.

Later, my chief administrator, Lisa Addeo, one of the firm's stalwarts, told me I no longer had an account open with Goldman Sachs. All of the accounts the firm had maintained were closed as of the last day of the year, when we went out of business. "What do I do?" the broker had asked Lisa when he got her on the phone. "He gave me all these orders but you do not have an account. They've all been closed."

"Then open one up!" she said. "This is Michael Steinhardt, for God's sake. He's trading. That's what he does. Anyway, whatever orders he put in, you know he's good for the money."

Within weeks, I had hired a trader, Chaim Rosenberg, to work with me to execute trades. I had been trading markets since I was 13. I guess I was not going to stop, not even in retirement.

∞

I also began investing my personal money with a diversified group of managers. It is primarily a portfolio of hedge funds, and while I try to keep a tight cadre of core managers, the list is probably too long. Many of these managers had worked for Steinhardt or had run money for us when we were active. In my geriatric period, investment goals have become conservative. I seek to achieve a mid-teen average annual return with relatively low volatility. Indeed, I hope never to lose money in any year. I am relatively insensitive to market benchmarks, and I opt toward moderate, safe, absolute returns.

After retiring, I sometimes read about how the stock market was on the verge of impending disaster in part because so many virgin investors, young analysts, and portfolio managers were on the Street, and they had not been around long enough to see the bust *and* the boom in the market cycles. I think there is some merit to this concern. Yet, another part of me remembered what it was like to be 26 years old, starting out on my own, and thinking I could conquer the world. Today, when I see that youthful spark in someone, I confess to being drawn to that person far more than to older and more experienced managers who are running billions and know with great confidence that financial history repeats itself. It may repeat but never in quite the same way, and, for sure, not when you are expecting it. I have also been around long enough to know that what has worked well in the past rarely continues to do so in the future.

Indeed, the recent growth in money management, particularly hedge funds, is astonishing. The best and the brightest as well as the less than the best and the less than the brightest seem to flock to Wall Street these days. I cannot help but think about the implications of this. Perhaps even more to the point, hedge funds, once managed and invested in by a select few, are anyone's game today. Whereas I once felt slightly uncomfortable justifying my fees, the horde of relatively undistinguished thirty-somethings who demand fees even higher than mine do not seem to give it much thought. Thus, adopting my usual contrarian view, I would be, at this time, figuratively short the hedge fund world.

What surprises me is that while I still find personal speculation in the markets rewarding, I have relatively little interest in the professional world of money management. For most of my life this was my intellectual preoccupation. Exploring the nuances of a field so rich in cerebral possibility used to be quite fulfilling. Now, however, money manager talk bores me. Perhaps this is not unusual, but, while I was in the business, my social relationships overwhelmingly included others in the financial world. Over time, relatively few friends from Wall Street have remained in my social sphere. Sometimes, when I am part of a conversation about the markets, I feel déjà vu and seek to change the subject. However, little was as egotistically rewarding as having great performance in markets. That is almost a distant memory.

Since 1995, I have continued to trade, although somewhat sporadically. For me, the instinct to trade is an addiction, and while I am in rehabilitation, I am not fully cured. I do not use a great deal of capital, with a few noteworthy exceptions. It seems my real goal is the creation of anxiety rather than making money. At that, I have been quite successful.

# 16

# THE DEATH OF
# MY FATHER

**F**OR MOST OF HIS LIFE, MY FATHER HAD BEEN robust, active, and outgoing. I saw him as a tough Damon Runyon character who could walk on Forty-seventh Street in the jewelry district where he worked for so many years, or on Broadway in the evening, and his fellow gamblers, wise guys, Hasidic Jews, and fancy babes would greet him as if he were an old friend.

But my father also had a softer side. He felt strong affection for his mother and had carefully arranged that, when the time came, he would be buried near her. He visited her grave every year. He was extraordinarily generous to his full brother and sister, as well as to other family members. Money was a tool for him; he loved to spend it. Giving people gifts—sometimes forcing expensive things upon them—was his greatest pleasure. He did so a bit ostentatiously on occasion. When I would go to the cemetery with him to visit his mother's grave, there was a religious old man who said a prayer for those who came to visit their loved ones. The usual compensation the man received was $5, or $10 at most, but my father gave him a $100 bill. Such generosity was clear for all to see.

My father loomed larger than life to me, even through my adulthood. He remained busy in the first years after he moved

251

to Las Vegas when he was 70 years old. He bought a spacious Spanish-colonial-style house in a residential neighborhood on the outskirts of Las Vegas. All of the houses had swimming pools in the backyards. He lived there with Susan Gyro, who had been a friend for many years, and, although he was far from being an easy companion, on balance they were happy.

In his retirement, my father lived on the money he had made as a jeweler, as well as the money he earned through my investments. During his later years, he was affluent relative to his peers and was always the first person to pick up the check. He had chosen to move to Las Vegas because he still gambled, knew many of the older players, and had a great camaraderie with them. They loved to sit in the casinos' lounges and tell stories about their memorable wins and their even more memorable losses. They would reminisce about the way "Vegas" used to be, with the "comps" and personal relationships, before the current corporate atmosphere brought changes.

My father went to the casinos every day. Truly, he had a love/hate relationship with gambling. He lost far more often than he won. Indeed, over the years, my father's net losses were in the millions, but that never stopped him from betting. In fact, it motivated him to try different approaches. He was constantly analyzing various techniques and strategies. There had to be some way for him, if not to beat the odds, then at least to improve them. Toward the end of his life, frustrated with losses, he settled on a technique. He would go into a casino and make three (but no more than three) large bets. If he lost, he would walk away, but only sometimes did he have the discipline to do that. He bet only three times because he believed that the fewer bets he made, the less the odds were against him. Sometimes, he and Susan would spend hours at the slots, where he could not do too much damage.

Wagering on sports was another favorite pastime. My father watched baseball, football, basketball, and boxing, but he cared about these events only if he had placed a bet. Speaking to him at least once a week, I could tell by his mood how many sports bets he had made and how many of those bets he had lost. His losses were extraordinary. One could have gotten rich by betting against him. His friends told me that he once got so angry when he lost in the last minute of a basketball game that he kicked his television set in. I remembered when we would be watching a football game on television. Losing his bet in the last few minutes of the game would make him furious. The frequency with which this happened was astonishing. He would be ahead for much of the game and then would lose by a point or two at the end. This was painfully consistent. For my father, gambling was a financial fiasco. Still, he kept at it, as only someone addicted could.

❧

Through his first few years living in Las Vegas, my father maintained a full life. He visited the casinos, went out socially, and traveled. He especially liked going to Santa Monica, California, where he would rent a hotel room near the beach and take long walks along the Pacific Ocean. He adored the California weather. He could spend hours sitting near the Santa Monica Pier, feeding the birds.

In his eightieth year, my father's health began to decline. Because I knew how energetic he was, it was hard for me to watch him deteriorate. All at once, his problems multiplied. A lymphoma treated a few years earlier recurred; he had macular degeneration that left him almost blind. His chronic hearing problem deteriorated to near deafness. He developed shingles, which became so bad that he was unable to shave the left side of his face for the last four years of his life. And, he had prostate cancer.

My father would often refer to the phrase "the golden years" with his wry cynicism. He would say, in his raspiest voice, "The golden years, what golden years? It's all bullshit."

My father's friends would tell me how proud he was of me, although I never heard my father say so himself. He saved his compliments for conversations with others. Friends let me know how much he loved his grandchildren, which I especially enjoyed hearing. With me, he was erratic. He would regularly ask me how much I was worth, and he seemed to take genuine pleasure in the number I told him.

More often than not, my father would be critical of me. He regularly claimed that, in the business dealings we had had over the years, I had not given him enough in return. When he was in this mood, he would say I did not appreciate how he had "staked" me early in my career. I guess he *had* staked me. By providing me with large sums of money to invest during those first years, he had allowed me to build up my own assets. But I always paid him well in excess of what he was due.

He seemed to be more and more defeated by his array of ailments. In his mid-80s, his white-blood-cell count was too high, and his prostate gave him pain. His extreme distrust of the medical profession complicated his condition. It was not unusual for him to be in a hospital where, if he felt frustrated, he would literally rip—I mean rip—the tubes out of his arms and walk out. He hated hospitals, hated confinement, and became outraged if a doctor kept him waiting for more than five minutes.

The last time I saw my father was about a month before he died. I had flown to Las Vegas, as I had done many times before, but this trip was especially difficult. That his condition had deteriorated was clear the moment I saw him. His energy level was low. He could see almost nothing. He could barely hear, which meant I had to shout at him, but even then only on his left side because he was totally deaf in his right ear. Most disturbing of all, he was often in excruciating pain. It hurt me to be in the same room with him and watch him suffer.

Susan had done a wonderful job of caring for him. My father needed constant attention, and she was unable to find good help to ameliorate her burden. He did not take well to others ministering to him even if it was in his interest. Susan looked exhausted. I felt sympathy, appreciation, and perhaps a little helpless. Susan loved my father and manifested it in her deep commitment to caring for him so well at this difficult time.

On this trip, he talked about our past relationship. As he lay in bed, he was so frail; he looked like the ghost of the man he once was. My father repeated what he had told me many times before. He had done his best, he said, in his weak, paper-thin voice. "We all make mistakes in life," he went on, "and we do things we regret. I know it was hard for you to show your affection for me. That bothers me, Michael. That bothers me a lot. But I did the best I could do in my life. I did the best I could do." Even at that point, I could not bring myself to tell him that I loved him. I just listened sympathetically.

In the final years of his life, I had forced myself to visit him as often as I could. I had pushed myself to keep in contact with him on a more regular basis than ever before. But I had done this out of a sense of obligation. I saw him because it was the right thing to do. I wish affection for my father had come more naturally to me.

Perhaps the flaws in my relationship with my father affected the way I dealt with my own children. With each of my kids, I feel boundless love. Did I show it as much as I should have? I was sensitive to my role as a father; at times, I consciously compared myself to my father. Fathers have sons who then become fathers; with my sons, I was harsher than I wish I had been. I would fret about my ability to control my temper.

∞

In the late summer of 1999, Judy and I went on a short vacation to the south of France. My father had been sick for so long, and death had seemed so close for so long, we had no sense that he was any closer to the end than he had been for months. We returned to our hotel room from a long walk one afternoon, and discovered 15 phone messages from our children. Judy knew instantly that something had happened. When I reached David, he told me that my father had passed away. Susan had rushed him to a hospital in Las Vegas, and he died quietly. I am not sure which illness killed him. It was probably a combination of them all.

Judy and I flew to New York to prepare for the funeral. We had my father's body flown back from Las Vegas so he could be buried beside his mother in a cemetery in Queens. Our children had made almost all of the preparations before we arrived. On the morning of August 5, we held a funeral service at the Riverside Chapel on the Upper West Side of Manhattan, not all that far from the Greystone Hotel where he had lived on and off throughout his life. I knew I still had inchoate and conflicting thoughts and emotions about my father, even after his death, but I decided to write a eulogy. Surprisingly, the writing came easily; what I would say about this monumental figure in my life flowed freely. On the day of his funeral, however, when it was time for me to walk to the front of the chapel and read the eulogy, I could barely control my emotions. Finally, as I stood at the lectern and looked out, I thought about my father—how much he had meant to me, and how much *more* he could have meant. I broke down weeping before I could say a word.

I cried uncontrollably, an experience I had never before had. How I had longed for him to be the father I wanted him to be. How, as a young boy growing up in Brooklyn, I had lain awake in bed at night and wondered what I had done *not* to have a father, like the other kids. How I had tried to make myself love him but realized I could not feel for him an unqualified love. Ambiguity remained.

I cried for some time, longer than I realized. Then I composed myself. I stared down at the white sheets of paper. Calmly, I read, "If one can be both, my father was 'one of a kind' and 'last of his kind,'" I began. "His was the chronicle of the Jewish experience in the twentieth century in America. He came from a background of poverty, he left school at the age of 12 to work at putting up awnings, he was one of nine and the last of these nine to leave this Earth."

I paused before I continued. "It may sound like a cliché, but my father was truly his own man. For most of his life, he did what he wanted, where he wanted, when he wanted. He suffered far fewer constraints than most of us, and that is what made him so distinct a character; he was a person one did not easily forget."

As I looked at the papers, they shook slightly in my hand. "For good and for bad," I went on, "he took chances. He gambled from very early in life, almost to the end. It was clearly an addiction. And it shaped him profoundly, in his personal relationships, business, and lifeview. I know that, at times, he wished he did not gamble but . . ."

I moved on to the personal. "My father was always generous—indeed, exceptionally generous. Most notably, with me. He was there for me when it counted. Because of him, I became interested in the stock market. Because of him, I went to Penn, which otherwise was not on my radar screen. Because of him, I got my start in investing, and the courage to start my firm at a very early age."

I tried to sum him up as a character. "It was of great importance to my father to be good and to do good," I read. "He was a character out of the *Guys and Dolls* era. He was a 'Reuta,' he was 'Red McGee.' My father was the terror of the Forty-seventh Street Jewelry District. He was the ultimate cash buyer, the risk taker. He used colorful language and expressions. 'Do not complain, do not explain,' he would say. He was unique."

Then I talked about family. "He loved his grandchildren and his great grandchild," I said. "Sara, my grandson Jacob, and I visited my father a few months ago. My father and baby Jacob were in bed together and he was truly happy. On the last day in the hospital, he called out for his grandson Danny, and the last person he asked for was his grandson David.

"But he also said to get the baby, baby Jacob, a Jewish star. A Jewish star with diamonds.

"That was my father, a Jewish star with diamonds."

After the funeral, we held a brief service for my father at the graveside. Then he was buried. It was an end of sorts. It could not, however, represent an absolute end because I still see him sometimes when I look in the mirror, particularly when I have a stubby beard, or in profile with my belly protruding. Or I hear him when Daniel imitates his gruff voice. He will always be with me.

⟨✕⟩

In the summer of 1999, we moved my mother into The Hebrew Home for the Aged, in Riverdale, New York. My mother had lived a relatively independent life until then. She had her own home in Margate, Florida, in which she lived alone for years after her husband Mark died in 1979. For most of the time, she had full-time help of high quality, and with these companions she remained on her own. She enjoyed shopping, always seeking the opportunity to find clothes for her grandchildren. She cooked for herself. She had a lively social life, often going out with her friends and relatives to local restaurants.

For the longest time, even though she did have a mild stroke, she remained remarkably intelligent, good-spirited, and optimistic. She had been that way all of her life. She would visit us in Bedford several times a year, and she and Judy would make jam from our fruit. We all looked forward to her visits.

In 1998, she started to deteriorate. I knew there was trouble when I visited her and she began talking about imaginary figures, people walking around outside her house. I asked her, "Where are these figures? *Who* are these people?" She would look outside and say, "These people out there." She could see them, but there were no people there.

Before long, my mother was diagnosed as suffering from Alzheimer's disease. In her case, she started to have trouble focusing and, as many Alzheimer's patients do, she sometimes lashed out, in frustration, at people around her. Most of the time, she was cogent, and it seemed worthwhile for her to remain independent in Florida, where she was most comfortable and familiar. That is what she wanted. We kept her there, hoping her around-the-clock help could manage her. Usually, she was fine. She was sufficiently social and she kept up a good patter. The deterioration progressed; yet, for a while, it was not so bad as to obstruct her lifestyle. We listened carefully to the women who cared for her, and we evaluated her problems. Medically, there was little to be done. Eventually, the woman upon whom we depended most told us she could not do the home care anymore. My mother had become too difficult to deal with. We then moved her to Riverdale, where she would be close to us.

She is there today; it is the best place for her. Even so, I feel guilt because she is not happy. There is nothing I can do to change that. I have to force myself to visit her. My trips there are painful. She recognizes me, and Judy, and a few others. She can talk with full knowledge of who I am, but mostly, she goes on and on disjointedly. Sometimes, with clarity, she asks me, "When am I going home?"

# 17

# TWO RIVERS

**I**N LOOKING BACK ON MY CAREER AND MY LIFE, I can see that my values, and the goals I continue to strive for, represent the confluence of two great rivers: the age-old river of Judaism, the people and the tradition, and the river of secularized America. From the Eastern European Jewish river flows a religion, and, more importantly, a culture, while from the other river flows twentieth- and twenty-first century American life with its openness, social mobility, and material prosperity. I believe my generation of Jews, in particular, is the product of these same two rivers, and the currents of both are strong within us. But, over time, the American river has grown stronger, becoming dominant in our lives, while the Eastern European river has been subsumed. For the first 50-plus years of my life, I too traveled, almost exclusively, along the secular river of American culture. Now I work, almost exclusively, on strengthening the flow of the river of my heritage.

Like many Jews of my generation, I was captivated as a youngster by role models who became successfully integrated into American culture through politics, business, entertainment, and sports. Supreme Court Justices Louis Brandeis and Felix Frankfurter, New York Governor Herbert Lehman, and financial titan Bernard Baruch were all names I took pride in as a young American Jew. Sid Gordon, third baseman for the New York Giants, and Sandy Koufax, from Lafayette High School, where I graduated, were childhood heroes. Others were not so overtly Jewish. I knew that Douglas Dillon, the Secretary of the Treasury in the Kennedy Administration, had a Jewish background as did Kirk Douglas. I knew Lauren Bacall is Jewish, and I knew Tony Curtis's real name is Bernie Schwartz. In the larger culture, there were constraints and quotas and a distant anti-Semitism, but I felt no limitations in my own life.

Today, American Jews are highly assimilated—so much so that it is often difficult for Jews to recognize their coreligionists in many common contexts particularly among todays' youth. Each generation moves farther away from their roots. Many of the values I have today came from the growing American river, but the Eastern European river of my heritage played an important role in who I became. Because of my success in America's secular world, I am in a position to try to help rebuild the strength of Jewish roots in America.

∞

After I retired from the markets, a new passion consumed me: the Jewish future. In America, most Jewish philanthropy is backward-looking. The overwhelming focus is on the past. Jews are impacted emotionally by the Holocaust and fears of anti-Semitism. Jews are inspired, as they should be, by the miracle of the birth of the State of Israel and the extraordinary sagas that immortalized its early years. However, for younger people, these events are almost ancient history hardly resonant in contemporary lives. I intend the focus of my philanthropy to acknowledge the extraordinary contributions of the past and to link them to a newly exciting future.

In 1994, before I retired, I created the Jewish Life Network. Its goal is to help American Jewry flourish in a fully integrated and open society. The Jewish Life Network seeks to revitalize Jewish identity through educational, religious, and cultural initiatives designed to reach out to the broadest community, with an emphasis on those who live near the margins of Jewish life. It is these non-Orthodox Jews who lead secular lives (albeit members of other denominations), the overwhelming majority of Jews in America, who must be reached if we are to effect a true renaissance.

The world now has only two areas in which there remain a meaningful Jewish population and a vigorous culture: Israel and North America. In these two areas live 80 percent of the world's Jewish population. Moreover, the number of Jews outside Israel is dwindling. Indeed, relative to the total population in the past 2,000 years, there have never been as few Jews on earth as there are today. Aside from Germany, no Diaspora country has generated population growth. We are not about to disappear, but the circumstance of our people is one of increased vulnerability that is not fully recognized. We Jews have never been about numbers, but at some point numbers begin to matter.

In the past 10 to 15 years, Holocaust memorials have sprung up in most major cities in the Western world. There has been an almost universal effort to capture that unspeakable time in Jewish history for future generations. The Jewish community has dwelled upon commemorating the awful experiences in its past, but has not figured out how to communicate the virtues and excitement of our heritage. Let there be no illusions. We are in crisis. Judaism, the cultural goose that laid so many golden eggs of Jewish achievement, far beyond any reasonable expectation, is in danger.

After my retirement, I thought about what I might pursue to respond to this crisis. I realized that Jews are immersed in the secular river of America for good. We are not going to withdraw from American life. An open society is the only choice for most of us. But we must accept the challenge posed by this freedom. The ultra-Orthodox alternative is based on insulation, isolation, and a belief in the superiority of the Jews. I respect such an alternative. Living that lifestyle is certainly the privilege of the Orthodox, and I find certain aspects of it very appealing, but it is not a serious option for most Jews. The result of the Jewish transformation in America, through which we have recently lived and are still living, is the wealthiest, highest-achieving Jewish community of all time, with unparalleled access to power and influence. Those Jews who were prepared to enter deeply into American society have done the best of all. As a result, 90 percent or more of American Jewry remains committed to full integration into the American lifestyle. To save this mainstream of Jewry, we must develop a way of life that flourishes distinctively while remaining fully integrated. That task is not easy.

Continuation of the status quo will lead us down the road to oblivion. So the question is: When you're playing a losing game, what do you do? I decided that my focus would be shaped by my projections of the Jewish future. I would commit myself to innovation as a philanthropic priority. Ideally, this would mean not just supporting new programs but also underwriting paradigm shifts. I want to change the Jewish community's capacity to reach groups that are falling out of its orbit.

I link this commitment to innovation with a second, related principle: entrepreneurial philanthropy. It seems clear that I should act in philanthropy as I did in business. Entrepreneurs do not accept the status quo or invest in safe bets. They create new instruments that generate new markets and change the state of the art. Entrepreneurs are willing to take a meaningful position in a company to ensure that it succeeds; they will even take a controlling interest to make sure the company works. In *tzedakah* (philanthropy), this would mean one must be willing to be a major, primary, or even sole supporter who makes a worthy project happen. Entrepreneurs risk failure—and indeed, sometimes fail—for the sake of great gain, but they put their judgment, time, and money into a project to ensure its success. I feel these principles should apply to philanthropy.

Because I have devoted so much of my time, energy, and money to the Jewish future, many people have accused me of being a closet believer. After all, how can an atheist devote himself to a cause that, by most definitions, is religious? Some part of me would like to believe in God, and I have gone to great lengths to find a theology with which I could be comfortable, but I have not found one. That is not to imply I do not lead a spiritual life; I do. I work at that part of myself, but, so far, I have not found a reason to take God as more than a metaphor. I also say that I am an atheist because I think being an atheist while believing firmly in the virtue of Jewish values, and associating myself with the history and the future of the Jewish people, could be an example to others who are also struggling with the issue of theology. Indeed there is a great tradition of Jewish atheism. Spinoza, Freud, and Einstein are just a few of a long and illustrious group.

Atheism or secular Judaism works for me. I would not try to impose my beliefs on anyone else, and I don't think people who believe otherwise are wrong. In fact, I admire them and, to a degree, I even envy them their faith. Aside from the issue of faith, the lifestyle and the community that I find most appealing is that of the modern Orthodox. There is a comfort that comes from a belief in God. I respect people who believe so strongly that belief has become an important element in their lives, a guide to the right way of living. For me, spiritual life consists of doing what I can for others. My Jewish identity has to do with a shared set of values, a place in a culture that has lasted 4,000 years, and a desire to reinvigorate its glories.

"Jewish values" is a phrase often heard but rarely defined. Sometimes this phrase is used to suggest good or elevated values that originate in the prophetic text of the Bible, but this usually results in an amorphous definition that does not distinguish Jewish ideals from others. For me, the concept of *tzedakah,* the *responsibility* for providing for society's weakest and least able was possibly unique to the Jews and continues with us, as does the belief in "social justice." Meritocracy is also grounded in the Biblical concept of the intrinsic dignity of every individual and is another treasured part of the Jewish tradition that has shaped my life and helped nurture my Jewish pride.

Yossi Beilin, the ex-Minister of Justice for Israel with whom I have often argued, believes there is no such thing as Jewish values. Values, he says are too much the product of a time and place, both of which are always changing. He would say that Jews only have their history in common. This is a worthy point, but history and values are, if not inseparable, intimately related.

One ancient and universal Jewish ideal is *Shabbat,* the tradition of one day being separated from the rest of the week for personal, familial, and nonremunerative activity. Some will consider its celebration religious but, for many, it transcends religion and has become the most important tradition in Jewish family life.

We are now living in a time of enormous change. Jews have always been a people of hope. The Talmud teaches that on Tisha B'Av, the day of our greatest historical catastrophe before the Holocaust, the Messiah will be born. My generation, which witnessed the Holocaust, also witnessed the creation of the state of Israel. But many American Jews have been assimilated and, in the process, have lost some of their Jewish identity. In this time of assimilation, we should set as our philanthropic goal the creation of a visionary and far-reaching renaissance of the Jewish soul and the Jewish community.

∞

I began to formulate an approach that would reach young secular Jews who were presently outside the framework of the community. A center was opened named Makor (Hebrew for "the source") aimed at Jewish professionals in their 20s and 30s, who were living in New York City. I embarked upon renovating a beautiful, five-story landmark building on West Sixty-seventh Street. It was to be a place where people could participate in activities they presently enjoyed. It would be a refuge of sorts, a place where young Jews living in the secular world could meet people who shared their culture and religious beliefs. In the building, we would have classrooms, lecture rooms, a theater, a terrace on which to socialize during the spring and summer, and a kosher café and bar on its lower level.

We decided to place no restrictions on who could come into Makor. Most Jewish organizations label themselves as "for Jews only," but we decided that highly integrated Jews would be turned off by that rule. This "open admissions" policy has been criticized by some bystanders but reflects the commitment of Jewish Life Network and me to enrich Jews who are fully integrated into the culture. There has been, as expected, a self-selection process, and we estimate that about 80 percent of Makor's constituency is Jewish.

Because young Jews are disproportionately involved as creators, Makor is on the cutting edge in culture and arts. There are specialized groups for budding filmmakers, playwrights, musicians, poets, and so on to share their works with others at the beginning stages of their careers. Moreover, Makor's Jewish resources can be called upon to enrich their works; the Jewish programming is "no holds barred." Only such programs can compete with the excitement of other opportunities in the wider culture.

Initially, we met with some resistance from neighbors who were concerned about having increased noise and traffic on an already busy street. In the end, we persuaded the zoning board that the center would not negatively affect the neighborhood, and we got permission to begin the renovation. Makor was opened to the public in 1999. From that day on, Makor has been an unmitigated success. The number of attendees has grown regularly. Its mailing list now exceeds 25,000, and it has truly become part of New York's cultural scene. I felt that my contribution had been made by the vision and funding, and Makor, over the long term, would be strengthened by being part of one of the greatest Jewish cultural institutions—the Ninety-second Street YMHA. In 2001, I gifted Makor to the YMHA, clearly assuring continuity of its programming magic. I am proud that my daughter Sara will become the next chairperson of its board.

Partnership for Excellence in Jewish Education, another group I founded, provides matching funds of up to $500,000 to any community that establishes a new Jewish day school. Virtually 100 percent of Orthodox children attend day schools. We hope to importantly increase the non-Orthodox numbers that currently represent just 10 percent of the constituency. Only 100 non-Orthodox day schools exist in the entire country, but this number has begun to grow.

Moreover, we would develop an approach that would offer expertise to any day schools that requested it, and would study ways to deal with the severe teacher shortage. The Jewish "civil service" world is in desperate need of upgrading. Only one national Jewish organization is experiencing powerful growth: the Hillel Foundation, of which I am co-chairman. Hillel, the Jewish address on most campuses, is run by a very capable leader, Richard Joel. With his guidance we started the Jewish Campus Service Corps, an organization that, each year, recruits 80 or so interns who introduce students to "doing Jewish" on campus.

With Judy, I also set up the Steinhardt Family Foundation in Jerusalem, which is run by Shula Navon, and supports worthwhile children's causes. Shula, one of Judy's and my dearest friends, my "Queen of Jerusalem," who spent almost 30 years working for the ill-tempered mayor of Jerusalem, Teddy Kollek, now finds herself working with the ill-tempered Michael Steinhardt. Teddy and I both appreciate her wisdom.

I hope that my career as a money manager will not dominate my epitaph. I do not get the level of fulfillment that many people do from such an achievement, even though it has been my most notable accomplishment outside of my family. The epitaph I *would* rather have is that I helped reinvigorate the non-Orthodox Jewish community in America. For now, I have a scant basis for justifying that, but most of my present energies extend in that direction. And these are the efforts that I will continue to pursue.

∞

In the spring of 1999, Judy and I were invited to Buckingham Palace to attend a charitable evening for the Israel Philharmonic Orchestra. We were full of anticipation as we sat in the back of our limousine that night in March, and made our way through London traffic. In a few minutes, His Royal Highness, Prince Philip, Duke of Edinburgh, would be greeting us, and 250 or so other guests, in the Bow Room. Judy assumed the Bow Room had gotten its name because it was where people bow to the royal family. She regretted that she had neglected to bring her white kid gloves, which she had not worn since high school, so she could make a proper curtsy before the husband of Queen Elizabeth II.

We forged ahead bare-handed and were relieved to discover that the "Bow" in the Bow Room referred not to the posture of visitors but to the marvelous windows, shaped like the bow of a ship. In any case, the bowing and scraping were kept to a minimum, and the mood was superb. After being introduced to the 77-year-old prince, I learned that we shared an interest in wild animals. Prince Philip was president of the World Wildlife Fund, and we talked for a few minutes about the importance of preserving endangered species.

Since we had gathered to hear Israel's premier orchestra, I had assumed most of the guests that evening would be Jewish. At one point, I struck up a conversation with a man named Chichester. My experience with British Jews had taught me that many of them do not have what Americans think of as typical Jewish names; there are plenty of Jewish Nigels and Conrads. I was in an effusive mood so I asked him where he had picked up such an Anglo-Saxon moniker. Chichester did not answer my question directly, and I thought he might be a bit embarrassed by my broaching the topic. To make him feel at ease, I said, "Mr. Chichester, what I think we should do tonight is trade identities. You take on my name and I'll take yours." He seemed amused, told me his first name was John, and said he would see me after the concert.

Following the reception in the Bow Room, we were ushered into a grand, high-ceilinged hall to hear the Israel Philharmonic Orchestra. During the interminable wait for Prince Philip to join us, I glanced at the guest list in the program. I had been mistaken about my assumptions concerning the religious makeup of the audience. I was embarrassed to see that "Mr. Chichester" was the Earl of Chichester, not some anglicizing Semite.

On a more serious note, I was also thinking about how pleased I was to be at what would be the premier performance of the Israel Philharmonic, founded as the Palestine Orchestra in 1936, at the official London residence of the monarchs who had had a mandate to govern the land that became the Jewish state. When the prince and his entourage finally entered, we all stood as the orchestra played the first four bars of "God

Save the Queen." While we were still standing, the Israel Philharmonic played "Hatikva," perhaps the first rendition of the
Israeli national anthem in Buckingham Palace.

The concert was superb. When it ended, the crowd dis-
persed into several rooms for a dinner. As we ate, I recalled
the attitudes of the British royal family toward Jews over the
years. I thought about the Nazi leanings of the Duke of Wind-
sor. But on this evening, those days seemed to be in the distant
past, as were the days of the British mandate in Palestine.
Though I still could remember certain strands of Mozart, in
the warmth of the moment a Hebrew saying came to my
mind: *"Hinei ma tov uma na'im shevet achim gam yachad"* ("Behold
how good and pleasant for brothers to be together"). Here in
the home of England's Queen.

∞

I have derived the most satisfaction from my most ambitious re-
vitalization project "birthright israel." This project has allowed
me to put into play all the principles that I believe philanthropy,
especially Jewish philanthropy, should employ, including a commitment to innovation and entrepreneurship. At the same time,
this project allows me to restore the strength of the Jewish river
of my heritage without diminishing the American river from
which American Jews, including myself, have gained so much.
This was accomplished with the creation of "birthright israel."

I am of a generation that has had a strong allegiance to Israel. For much of my life, I was able to substitute Israel for theology; it was easy for me to idealize the creation of the State of
Israel as a miracle that would take its place among the greatest
events in Jewish history. Memory fades fast, however. My
children know Israel only as a maturing nation that is no
longer the underdog that it once was. They do not have the
same emotional connection with Israel, and they are not alone
in their detachment. The next generation of American Jews

will hardly relate to Israel with the intensity that my generation has. An extraordinary gap will not be easily filled, except in dire circumstances, and those, I hope, we will never see. One sometimes hears that America and its vaunted Jewish citizens can be counted on in case of an emergency situation in Israel. That was true 30 or 40 years ago, but I am not so confident that it will be the case in the future.

Over the years, many efforts have focused on enhancing the relationship between American Jews and Israel, but, so far, these attempts have not achieved much. There is also little reason to be optimistic about enhanced relationships between the Jews of Israel and the declining Diaspora. Thus, Israel's role as an important foundation for American Jews remaining Jewish is increasingly dubious.

In the spring of 1997, Judy and I attended a fund-raising ball at the Israel Museum in Jerusalem. I ran into Charles Bronfman (and his wife Andy), whose family controlled The Seagram Company. For years, I had admired the work Charles had done through Israel Experience, an organization that had been responsible for bringing Jewish youth to Israel. At one time, the program had brought as many as 10,000 U.S. high school kids to Israel each year. Recently, the program had more or less leveled out.

I told Charles I wanted to talk. The two of us went outside to be alone. On a beautiful night in Jerusalem, sitting on a stone wall where we could see the lights of the city below, I proposed to Charles that we should try to create a universal trip whereby every Jew, aged 18 to 26 years, would have, as a rite of passage (the way Bar and Bat Mitzvahs have become a rite of passage in Jewish life), a 10-day trip to Israel. This trip would allow them to discover their Jewish heritage and spiritual homeland at a critical time in their coming of age.

"Let's do something very big and very audacious," Charles said at one point.

"That's exactly what we must do," I said. "We'll take your concept of Israel Experience and expand on it."

Charles agreed.

"I feel that I have made all of this money," I said, "but I have changed nothing. Together, we can make a difference."

"I couldn't agree with you more," Charles said. "When do we start?"

The plan we came up with was not unambiguous. Henceforth, the Jewish people would commit to offer every Jew born on Earth a universal gift: a free educational trip to Israel. The trip would include *mifgashim*—strong, personal encounters—between young Diaspora Jews and young Israeli Jews. This would hopefully foster relationships of binding souls together to make the Israel-Diaspora link memorable and meaningful. That evening in Jerusalem, Charles and I agreed that Israel, with all its problems, could be the cement to hold the world Jewish community together. We agreed to each put up $5 million to start developing an organization called "birthright israel."

It was one good way, we thought, to respond to a projection made for the World Jewish Congress. The projection stated that, within the next 30 years, the Jewish population outside of Israel, about eight million people as of now, could decline to about four million. This decline was due, in large part, to intermarriage. Half of all Jews were marrying non-Jews, and the children of a large segment of those intermarried couples were leaving the Jewish faith. Moreover, the Jewish population in places as diverse as Argentina, South Africa, and the former Soviet Union was expected to decline even more rapidly because of its aging population. Charles and I departed the party that evening encouraged by our new resolve. We hoped "birthright israel" would be an outstanding example of what can happen when two businessmen create an entrepreneurial philanthropic partnership.

By the summer of 1998, we had developed a plan that would fund "birthright israel." In Jerusalem, Prime Minister Benjamin Netanyahu announced he would commit $20 million a year to the project. The United Jewish Appeal/Council of Jewish Federations agreed to give $20 million a year. In addition, Charles and I said we would raise another $20 million a year on our own. The fund would then have $60 million a year with which to operate. Starting January 1, 2000, 15,000 college-aged Jews would be brought to Israel. In five years, that number would double.

The *New York Times* reported, in the fall of 1998: "In an attempt to rebuild religious identity among young Jews, who are marrying non-Jews and abandoning the faith in large numbers, Jewish organizations plan to start a program that will pay for any Jew in the world between age 15 and 26 to travel to Israel for 10 days. The program, 'birthright israel,' is expected to cost $300 million over five years and will be financed by the Israeli Government, a group of major Jewish donors from North America, and the Council of Jewish Federations."

I should point out that, from the start, "birthright israel" had its critics. Even today, some Jews question the impact a 10-day trip to Israel can have on a young adult's Jewishness. "Providing vast sums of money to youngsters, including many from affluent homes, for 10-day junkets without requiring any form of commitment is demeaning to Israel," Isi Leibler, the chairman of the board of the World Jewish Congress, wrote about "birthright israel" in the *Jerusalem Post*. "It is inconceivable that a 10-day trip can be the jump-off point for creating newly committed Jews."

Certain individuals in the Orthodox community argue that instead of sinking $60 million a year into "birthright israel," we should spend that money on day schools, because a day school has a more enduring impact on the lives of the children who attend it. Or, if not day schools, we should fund summer camps, again because camps may affect more youth more profoundly.

The critics do have a point. The fact is, however, for most non-Orthodox Jews in America—or in the Diaspora in general—day schools are not a part of their lives. These Jews do not send their children to day schools, not because they cannot afford the tuition, but because they *do not want to*. They believe in public education (or secular, private education) and, more to the point, they lead secular lives.

We developed "birthright israel" to reach out to those Jews, the "silent majority" of Diaspora Jews who are not involved in synagogues and who consider themselves cultural, not necessarily religious, Jews. Charles and I saw this as a chance to reinforce their Jewishness with a project they would see as accessible and appealing.

We felt so strongly about this project that, while lining up the support of the Israeli Government and the Jewish Federation, we went ahead—on our own—and put up the seed money needed to finance the first trip. In 1999, Charles and I each wrote a check for $9 million. With that $18 million, we began to put our plan into action.

First, we announced "birthright israel" in the summer of 1999. Applications were due in the fall. Hillel proved to be one of our best allies in the program. The number of applicants dwarfed our most optimistic expectations. To give just one example, for the 60 places we had allotted Cornell University, we received 400 applications. We had to hold a lottery to pick the 60 students who could go. The same situation developed at colleges and universities all across America.

Ultimately, our selection procedure gave us a group of some 6,000 college students from around the world. About 4,000 came from the United States and another 1,000 from Canada. We also picked 1,000 kids from 14 other countries, including Chile, Uruguay, Brazil, Argentina, England, France,

Australia, and the countries of the former Soviet Union–Georgia, Moldova, Uzbekistan, and Ukraine. Of the 4,000 Americans, 3,000 came from Hillel.

The flights to Jerusalem began in late December 1999. Judy and I flew over on January 3, 2000, on an El Al jet embossed with the "birthright israel" logo. We were traveling along with 388 "birthright israel" kids from a variety of American universities. There was no better way to have welcomed the new millennium than to go on this journey.

I stayed a full 10 days. The trip was clearly an intense experience for many of the kids. In the conversations I had with them, I heard only one complaint: they didn't have time to sleep. The sine qua non for each trip was at least one experience concerning the Holocaust; one about the birth of Israel; one devoted to Biblical Jewry; and one *mifgash,* an encounter where the kids spent time with Israeli peers who had more or less the same background.

Aside from these events, the kids individualized their trips. Most went to the Western Wall in Jerusalem. Some went to kibbutzim, some dug in archeological sites, and some visited classrooms. They met Israeli politicians and peace negotiators. They talked to Natan Sharansky, the courageous Russian dissident who became a minister in the government of Israel. They met immigrants from Russia and Ethiopia.

Israel, of course, is roughly the size of New Jersey, and two-thirds of it is desert. These kids had 10 days to explore an area of only that size, so they actually got to see much of the country. A number of them took Jeep trips and bicycle rides through the Golan Heights. By and large, most of them had never heard of the Golan Heights, but after having seen the topography, with vulnerable agricultural settlements situated below, they were absolutely opposed to giving up the Golan Heights in any peace negotiations. In a very real way, the Golan Heights became *theirs* simply by visiting. They developed a sense of ownership for this land that most of them had known nothing about prior to the trip.

As I ran into groups of "birthright israel" students on the street or at various events, I would stop them and ask how they were enjoying themselves. "Hi, are you from 'birthright israel?'" I would ask.

They would look at me curiously and answer, "Yes."

When they found out who I was, they were sincere in showing their gratitude. There was no cynicism at all. Their reactions were genuine and heartfelt. "I can't believe how much this has changed my life," I heard one after another say. It was beyond anything I had imagined. These were typical college kids and they were enthralled. They had been captured by the spirit of Israel.

Hearing the reactions made me feel wonderful. This was a meaningful way for them to become more invested in their Jewish heritage, to develop a more positive view of what it means to be a Jew, and to experience Jewish joy and excitement in a way they never had before. Their reactions made me realize that, in these 10 days, we had inspired a group of young people who would be more committed to their heritage. Their reactions also made me understand that if we could truly offer this trip universally, it could change the community forever.

On the last Saturday night of our trip, we had a gala, in the main convention center in Jerusalem, for 5,000 "birthright israel" participants. It was a marvelous moment as I looked out at this massive audience of young people. Charles and I were both slated to speak, and with the help of Rabbi Yitz Greenberg I had written a short speech that was a takeoff on the Gettysburg Address. The content of the speech was Jewish, but the speech's style was in the tradition of Lincoln.

"Four millennia ago, our ancestors brought forth on this earth a new people," I began, standing at the podium on the dais, in front of a hushed audience, "nurtured by the belief that every human being is created in the image of God, and dedicated to the principle of Tikkun Olam, of perfecting the world until it respects the infinite value, equality, and uniqueness of every person in that image."

I paused to look at the audience, all those young, attentive faces. "To advance our purpose," I continued, "we Jews have served as teachers to the world, sharing our Bible and Talmud, giving birth to Christianity, midwiving Islam and Western culture. Along the way, we have served as role models, offering our values of family and community, upholding our practice of *tzedakah* and responsibility for our fellow human beings. In this process, we have outlasted ancient, medieval, and modern civilizations. We have survived exile, expulsion, massacre, and Holocaust and outlived tyrants from Pharaoh and Haman to Stalin and Hitler."

I stopped briefly, caught up in the emotion I felt. "In the past few decades," I went on, "we have arisen from the ashes of Shoah and rebuilt our homeland, Israel. We have restored the value and dignity of Jewish life. We have come into freedom and acceptance and earned power and affluence as never before in human history. The price of these historic achievements has been erosion of our uniqueness and weakening of our ties as one people."

I continued, my voice filled with emotion. "We here must firmly resolve that all those who lived and died for Jewry shall not have lived and died in vain," I said. "We must promise that this people, in partnership with the living and the dead, with God and humanity, shall have a new birth of freedom. We must live our lives as witnesses, as teachers, as builders, so that the Torah of the Jewish people, the teaching by the Jewish people, the concern for the Jewish people, shall flourish again on this earth."

When I finished, I looked up to see this sea of young faces staring back at me. Dead silence filled the auditorium; not one sound, one motion. Then, all of a sudden, the kids started to applaud, quietly at first but soon louder. The sound of the applause became deafening and, just when it was the loudest, the kids started to stand. Before long, everyone in the room was on their feet applauding. As I stood on the stage, I could hardly control my emotions. I welled up inside and started to cry. It was a profoundly special moment, for I knew these kids had heard and understood their part in a four-millennium history. They represented the product of all the Jews who had lived and died before them.

I could also tell from their reaction that my speech had touched them deeply, which made all the work that had gone into the trip more than worthwhile. It was a singular moment in my life, an instant when I knew without question I had made a real difference in the lives of other people.

Later, after the program finished, numerous young people came up to me to express their gratitude. One young man could not stop crying. "I never believed I could experience something like this in my life," he said to me through his tears. "I never believed I could have this. I feel a connection to the Jews who have come before me that I didn't even know existed. I am so grateful to you, Mr. Steinhardt. I thank you from the bottom of my heart."

I knew then that our original concept for "birthright israel" was a good one and I resolved to make the project an ongoing reality. I will take the image of that young man's face, streaked with tears, with me for the rest of my life. I believe those tears represented the strong reunion of the two rivers of my life: a reinvigorated American Judaism.

# Index